DON'T LOOK DOWN

ANSWERING JESUS' CALL TO WALK ON THE WATER

Rosario Picardo

DISCIPLESHIP
RESOURCES

ISBNs
978-0-88177-919-6 (print)
978-0-88177-920-2 (mobi)
978-0-88177-921-9 (ePub)

Library of Congress Control Number: 2019932246

Cover design by GoreStudio, Inc.
Interior by PerfecType, Nashville, TN

DR919

CONTENTS

Introduction

What They Don't Teach Pastors

It was a dark and stormy night.

Imagine you are Peter. Out on the small fishing boat you feel relatively comfortable, even at home, despite the blackness, the wind, and the waves that would quickly put most non-fishermen on edge. While the waves rock the boat, you sit with the other disciples, fishing nets idle, and talk about the almost unbelievable miracle you saw earlier that day. You marvel at how Jesus miraculously fed thousands of people with just a few loaves of bread and some fish, the meager remnants of the meal that was more than ten times what they had started with. Afterward, Jesus had asked you and the others to go out on the boat and wait for him. Now, the energy and wonderment are almost palpable. What miraculous signs and wonders would tomorrow bring with this teacher? What were his plans for each of you?

Suddenly, a figure appears in the dark, walking toward you on the water as if it were soil. Your weary and excitable mind strains to make sense of the vision. What else could it be but a ghost? You and the others are terrified. As if in reply to your thoughts, a voice you recognize shouts out across the water, "Take courage! It is I. Don't be afraid." And at that moment you realize that it is none other than Jesus himself, standing on the surface of the water.

Something almost unknown rises up in you. With surprise, you find yourself standing and responding to Jesus. "Lord," you say, "if it's you, tell me to come to you on the water."

As if knowing the question before you asked it, Jesus bids you to come.

You stare back, focusing only on this man who performs miracles.

You step out of the boat. Standing on the water, not sinking.

You take a step. You walk. Toward Jesus.

You walk on the water. You're walking on water!

Your mind catches up to you as the realization hits. Walking on water? No one can walk on water! What is happening?! You look down. You take your eyes off of Jesus. You hear the wind and feel the sting of sea spray. It laughs at you, reminding you that you can't control the elements. In the sudden onset of fear, you almost forget Jesus completely, and you begin to sink.

You then remember Jesus, only yards away, and in terror you cry out to him. Immediately, Jesus reaches out his hand and catches you. "You of little faith," he says, "why did you doubt?"

Finally, safely back in the boat, you hear the wind die down.

The emotional and intellectual roller coaster Peter stepped onto that day went something like this:

Fear: How can we feed these people?

Hope: Jesus has a plan.

Astonishment: Jesus has used us to perform God's miracle!

Joy: Hallelujah!

Calm and questioning: Retreat in the boat. Curiosity about Jesus' actions and plans.

Intense fear: It's a ghost! In a dark storm miles from shore!

Crazy hope: No, it's Jesus, walking on the water!

Adrenaline-filled fear and excitement: Jesus will call me out to him!

Exhilaration: Jesus *can* call me out to him! Jesus has made the water like solid ground to my foot!

Focus: I see only Jesus and want to be near him.

Joy: In this moment, I trust in Jesus completely and act in that trust.

Terror: Wait, I *cannot* walk on the water! Oh, help me! What am I doing?

Relief: Jesus has caught me.

Gratefulness: Jesus will save me.

Shame: Why did I doubt Jesus?

Gratefulness: Jesus will save me.

Hope: What could Jesus do through me next time? And the next time? And the next?

Despite the tumult, most people would love to have an adventure like Peter's. Knowing how Peter's story unfolds, we would gladly accept the momentary fear in order to encounter the thrill and joy of Jesus' miracles taking place through us and around us. Indeed, this story is one of the Bible's strongest illustrations of acting in faith for Jesus.

Yet sometimes the story falls flat because we envision the disciples as devoid of our shared human psychology. The story of Peter walking on water isn't a quick, one-dimensional Sunday school lesson in trust and obedience. Rather, we see Peter struggle with, overcome, and again fall victim to patterns of thinking common to us all: a desire to control, to know, to manipulate, to run our own show; a reliance on our own understanding instead of accepting God's; a preference to be safe, unaware, or unbothered instead of tested and stretched in our faith and fulfilled in our purpose. Peter sheds these thinking patterns in order to experience Jesus' call for himself. When he does, he learns that Jesus equips him beyond his understanding—and that Jesus rescues him when he falls.

What we often fail to consider is that Jesus calls each of us onto the water every day of our lives. He is calling us right now! Of course, our story will look much different than Peter's, but we each have equal opportunity to experience and participate in God's awesome plans for us.

The truth is, most of us want a life-giving faith, but our daily habits turn into comfortable, unexamined ruts. When we're stuck—and, what's worse, when we're *okay with being stuck*—the reality is that we are willingly missing out on what God plans and wants to do in us and through us.

What if the first step out of the rut is to take a risk? Not a senseless risk, but a God-given risk, risking failure, possibly leaving behind comfort and complacency, even leaving what feels like safety or a previous calling in order to gain a far greater adventure?

This book encourages readers to long for and expect faith-filled adventure, to identify the metaphorical boats that God is calling each of us out of and the waters he is calling us onto. Throughout this book, we will follow ten people's stories as they have pushed away from shore, identified their boats, asked for God's call, heard God's call, stepped out on the water, and even begun sinking and were rescued by God. I have had the good fortune to be surrounded by many who live walk-on-the-water lives—so much so that it was difficult to choose which stories to write about! I chose the following stories for their ability to encourage me in my own faith walk. I hope you draw the same encouragement.

Rev. Dr. Angie Edwards

I first met Angie Edwards at a weekly preachers' team meeting in which we preview our sermons for the weekend. When Angie was introduced to me as Frank Thomas's sister, I was immediately intimidated because Frank Thomas is one of the most acclaimed and polished preachers in the country. Thankfully, Angie's calming presence put me at ease, and her insight was helpful and encouraging as she responded to my sermon for the upcoming weekend. Soon, Angie was no longer "Frank's sister" to me because I discovered her giftedness and anointing as a leader and preacher. Furthermore, as I got to know her story, I was encouraged through hearing how she overcame major obstacles, and I know you will be encouraged as well.

Tim Krug

I first met Tim Krug when we were partnered together to represent our church in London, England, to learn about The Alpha Program.

As Tim and I roomed together and shared meals and our stories, we became fast friends. I was inspired by what Tim had to overcome in his life and ministry. I was impressed by Tim's ministry to those on the margins of society and by his heart for the underdog.

Rudy Rasmus

I first heard Rudy speak at a conference called Change the World in 2012. I was mesmerized by his candor, humor, and directness. I'll never forget how he referred to his famous braided goatee: a "filter" is what Rudy called it because, he said, it helped him to find out whether someone he'd just met was judgmental or not. I identified with Rudy because I had done urban ministry for ten years and appreciated his perspective and influence at St. John's United Methodist Church in Houston, Texas. What I never would have guessed is that not long after, I received a call from United Theological Seminary's doctoral department asking me to lead a focus group—and Rudy was one of the group's students. Now, a few years later, Rudy has gone from being a mentor to being a good friend and a listener whom I can bounce ideas off of. Beyond that, Rudy is a calculated risk-taker, and he has taught me that God is never done calling us out of the boat to take the next steps, no matter how much God has already accomplished through us.

Jordan Wilson

One of the up-and-comers in a new generation of spiritual leaders is Jordan Wilson, who serves as Connections Coordinator for the Ginghamsburg Church campus, The Point, in Trotwood, Ohio. I first met Jordan when she visited The Point while she was a seminary student. Right away I recognized her eagerness to learn and relate to people. After our initial encounter, Jordan was placed with The Point for an internship.

Jason Moore

Years ago, I was asked to speak at a major conference in New England. It was one of the first conferences where

I was speaking, let alone keynoting. What could anybody learn from me? I wasn't a big name or a megachurch pastor. In short, I was terrified.

However, my nervousness turned into ease as I found out that I would be paired with another keynote speaker who was much more experienced. Jason Moore was helping to design the conference and the worship component, and he taught me valuable insights in the short conversations we had leading up to the conference. Little did I know that meeting Jason would later lead me to explore my calling to move to Dayton, Ohio, and to join the pastoral staff of Ginghamsburg Church, which happens to be Jason's home church. Jason has an entrepreneurial spirit and continues to challenge himself and others to think outside the box.

Tom and Sandy Bench

I first met Tom and Sandy a few years ago when they moved back to Trotwood, Ohio. I was intrigued by this older couple who had endless energy to serve the community through tutoring immigrants and refugees, helping in our food pantry, and serving as Sunday morning greeters. The biggest impact this couple has made on me is their humility. Tom comes by two to three times a week to pick up trash in our parking lot, and they both do landscaping in the flowerbeds. They are foundational in loving our community.

Chandi and Jamel

I first met Chandi and Jamel in church one day as they were visiting The Point. They were intrigued by the nonjudgmental and laid-back environment; they hadn't experienced this before in a local church. On their first Sunday, they sat next to a cousin they hadn't seen in years. Jamel's cousin fell on hard times and was staying at a local men's shelter. (The Point picks up men from this shelter and brings them to church.) This chance encounter with a cousin, in addition to the welcoming spirit of the church, told Chandi and Jamel they were in the right place and had found their church home. As I heard their story, I knew it could help other couples struggling in their relationships.

Callie Picardo

As a church planter who started with a congregation of exactly zero people in Lexington, Kentucky, I knew I needed to meet people. I didn't have an office, and, frankly, I didn't want one (which, incidentally, is why we are turning my current office into a prayer room).

For that reason, while in Lexington, I made Starbucks my office. One thing I learned immediately is that people didn't go to Starbucks for the overpriced drinks with Italian names; the patrons, even when hiding behind laptops and iPads, went there because they secretly wanted to be around others.

One day, while in the middle of back-to-back business meetings, I came across a young lady who worked for a nonprofit in charitable giving. She wanted to connect with our donors; I took her business card but didn't mention that, in fact, we had no donors! The reality was, I had an ulterior motive. This young woman was a Christian and happened to be quite attractive, and I wanted her contact info.

Shortly thereafter, I got in touch with her and set up what I thought was a date and what she thought was a business meeting. When she pulled out her business folder to go over what her nonprofit had to offer, my jaw dropped. I tried to steer the conversation to more personal questions, but she wasn't having it. When I learned that we had some mutual acquaintances, I devised a new strategy and set up a time to hang out with everybody. A lot of my attempts failed, but I was persistent, to say the least! She got the hint because I kept inviting her to different functions. I finally landed a date, and it was the best date I had ever been on. However, being the prayerful person she was, God gave her the red light. Meanwhile, I kept praying hard because I had not met anybody like her. Finally, God answered our prayers and we were married.

Callie's risk-taking ability has come from a deep spiritual foundation. She has been an inspiration to me in her devotion to God through prayer. Callie has helped me avoid making rash decisions and has encouraged me to put spiritual filters in place so that I don't chase my own selfish ambition into pitfalls. God has made us better together.

Chapter One

Pushing Away from Shore

Life is either a daring adventure or nothing.
—HELEN KELLER

Immediately Jesus made the disciples get into the boat and go on ahead of him to the other side, while he dismissed the crowd. After he had dismissed them, he went up on a mountainside by himself to pray. Later that night, he was there alone, and the boat was already a considerable distance from land, buffeted by the waves because the wind was against it.
—MATTHEW 14:22–24

Not knowing what lay ahead, the disciples must have been anticipating an upcoming adventure. They had just witnessed Jesus miraculously feed thousands of people with very little food. But then, Jesus had instructed the disciples to go out onto their boat at dusk, without him, to wait. The circumstances were less than ideal for taking such a risk. John 6:14–15 explains Jesus' urgency at making the disciples get into the boat without him: "After the people saw the sign Jesus performed, they began to say, 'Surely this is the Prophet who is to come into the world.' Jesus, knowing that they intended to come and make him king by force, withdrew again to a mountain by himself." Jesus made the disciples leave for protection and his own need for solitude.

Being sent away from Jesus must have been trying for the disciples after having witnessed one of the largest-scale miracles they would see in their discipleship and after the mayhem of Jesus needing to escape the crowds for self-protection. They may have been surprised by Jesus' desire for solitude. Could this have been a test to see how they would react? Would the disciples be obedient to this command, even though they'd be more comfortable staying in Jesus' presence?

Additionally, by the time Jesus began walking toward the disciples, the boat was far from shore—possibly three or four miles away. The weather wasn't cooperating and there were strong waves.[1] The word Matthew's Gospel uses to describe what the waves were doing to the boat is "buffeted," which can also be translated to "tormented." Interestingly, this word is used in connection with demonic activity in Matthew 8:6 and Revelation 9:5.[2]

The disciples may have felt some hesitation in the situation. Why did Jesus make them go out in the boat alone into the storm? He had just provided for a multitude of people, but what about his own disciples? Peter may also have been wondering this—and more—when Jesus called him to walk out on the water. And yet, Peter still believed that adventure was for him. He accepted the risk of leaving behind his immediate fear and trusting Jesus.

This expectation of adventure, even when we may be feeling confused or temporarily let down, is something we must cultivate in our own walk with God. God wants to use each of us in incredible ways. Sometimes we look at the adventures others have had and think, "That was a special task just for them. I don't have a role like that." Or maybe we think, "You don't know my past. You don't know my problems. You don't know my handicaps. I don't even like adventure." Yet, when we believe adventure *can* be for us, we awaken to God's calls in our lives.

Practically speaking, the expectation of adventure can look like a purposeful daily activation of faith. "God, I believe you are at work in my life today. I believe you have adventures planned for me this day." It can be looking for those unexpected opportunities that take us out of our comfort zone and place us fully in God's hands to find new ways to love others. It is also an ability to rest in our unknowing nature, expectantly waiting for God's nudge.

Like the disciples who were told to push away from shore in their boat—away from the comfort of Jesus' presence and his directions about what would come next—we do not know where God's plans will lead us. But we must practice faith that God's plans *do* include us. We must be satisfied that, though we can't see tomorrow, we are always a vessel of God's work. And we must expect to go out and meet the adventure when God calls.

As in many other aspects of our walk with Jesus, the act of pushing out to sea looks quite different than the way modern life is organized. Today's world offers dull routine: get up in the morning, have breakfast, drop the kids off at school, head to work, work all day, head home, pick the kids up, eat dinner, talk with the family, watch a little television, go to bed, then get up the next day and do it all again. The well-organized among us know what lies ahead on the calendar for weeks, if not months and even years, and we shape our actions to fit the routine. Is this life? A collection of days lived doing the same thing over and over again, more or less? Or maybe life is a compilation of plans made, carried out, modified, or abandoned?

In the movie *Groundhog Day*, the main character, Phil (played by Bill Murray), finds himself reliving the same day over and over again. At first Phil finds it amusing or even exciting as he can relive the same day, relying on others' predictable actions but experimenting with different crazy schemes or missions. Eventually, however, he becomes bored and, even worse, depressed. Everything becomes meaningless to him. As Phil is feeling sorry for himself in a bar, he asks, "What would you do if you were stuck in one place, and every day was the same, and nothing that you did mattered?" Another man at the bar responds, "That about sums it up for me."[3]

I wonder if that answer can best describe our feelings. We have lost our desire for fulfillment and purpose, and we don't venture outside the mundane life we are living on earth. It's easy to find our identity solely in our roles as a husband or wife, father or mother, or in our occupation. Indeed, when we meet someone, after exchanging our names and simple pleasantries, we often ask, "What is it that you do?" The expectation is that "what you do" refers to nothing beyond one's employment.

But what we all know is that life is more than your occupation. Life doesn't have to replay as a simple, daily routine. What you get paid to do is not necessarily what you were made for. Life is about adventure.

This doesn't mean that your day-to-day occupation cannot be a crucial springboard to ministry or calling. For example, the apostle Paul was a tent-maker who made garrison tents out of leather for the Roman army. Paul started out much of his ministry able to go in and out of the Gentile world because of his Roman citizenship and his skills. It was in his workshop that Paul was likely to have many spiritual discussions with customers and other people who were passing by. What Paul was getting paid for was not necessarily what he was made for.

Another example comes from one of the people I admire from the history of the church, a man by the name of Brother Lawrence. Lawrence was a seventeenth-century

Catholic monk who was a layperson. Lawrence wasn't necessarily educated, but it didn't matter. He spent almost all of his adult life within the walls of the monastery, first working in the kitchen, then as a repairer of sandals in his later years.

Despite his lowly position in life and at the monastery, his character attracted many to him. Lawrence had a reputation for experiencing profound peace, and several people came to visit him and seek his spiritual guidance. Lawrence spent most of his time washing dishes in the monastery as a service to God and often talking to God during a routine task that many people don't enjoy. It was in those moments as a dishwasher that Lawrence would encounter God. The wisdom and teachings that Lawrence passed on would later become the basis for his book, *The Practice of the Presence of God*. This book influenced not only many Catholics, but Protestants as well.

Lawrence's writing wasn't published until after his death. Lawrence didn't autograph a single copy, go on a book tour, or speak to thousands. Nonetheless, he had a profound influence on the trajectory of Christianity. Most notably, he influenced John Wesley, the founder of Methodism, which has 12 million members worldwide and 32,000 United Methodist churches in the United States.

The lesson here is not just that God may use our trade skills for Kingdom work, but also that our Kingdom work may not always *feel* like an adventure, *unless we're paying attention*!

What do you want out of life? Jesus asked his would-be disciples the same thing in John 1:35–39:

The next day John was there again with two of his disciples. When he saw Jesus passing by, he said, "Look, the Lamb of God!" When the two disciples heard him say this, they followed Jesus. Turning around, Jesus saw them following and asked, "What do you want?"

They said, "Rabbi" (which means "Teacher"), "where are you staying?" "Come," he replied, "and you will see." So, they went and saw where he was staying, and they spent that day with him.

The disciples respond to this all-important question, "What do you want?" by asking Jesus a question: "Where are you staying?"

I had always suspected that John's disciples (the ones Jesus asks) must have been caught so off-guard that their first response was to come up with a dumb question. If Jesus the Christ asked you what you were looking for, would you blurt out, "Well, what hotel are you staying at?" In Greek, however, the question's primary meaning translates less closely to "Whose house are you crashing at?" and more closely to "Where do you abide?" As in, "Where does your spirit live, Jesus? Where does your heart dwell?"

21

Intriguingly, Jesus does not answer directly but instead replies simply, "Come and see." He didn't pull up a PowerPoint to give a theology lecture. He wanted the disciples to learn by seeing and doing. The disciples must push away from shore in order to follow Jesus and learn his purpose and, ultimately, their own.

Similarly, Jesus speaks about the cost of discipleship in Luke 9:57–62:

———

As they were walking along the road, a man said to him, "I will follow you wherever you go."

Jesus replied, "Foxes have dens and birds have nests, but the Son of Man has no place to lay his head."

He said to another man, "Follow me."

But he replied, "Lord, first let me go and bury my father."

Jesus said to him, "Let the dead bury their own dead, but you go and proclaim the kingdom of God."

Still another said, "I will follow you, Lord; but first let me go back and say goodbye to my family."

Jesus replied, "No one who puts a hand to the plow and looks back is fit for service in the kingdom of God."

———

Few today are called to the life of itinerant ministry, healing, or miracle-working. Yet Jesus' point remains if we wish to follow his specific callings on our own lives. While a routine, a schedule, and organized plans are not in themselves prohibitive in our faith walk, in order to accept the adventure God calls us to, we must be always willing to set aside our plans and supposed foreknowledge of the day ahead.

To some, pushing away from shore is an unsettling feeling of waiting for God's next move. For others, it is the anticipation of something new and exciting on the horizon. Often, pushing away from shore is a time to build new skills; acknowledge or learn about God-given strengths; and understand areas, circumstances, or people God may soon call you to.

Early on in my ministry, my first staff position at a church was actually as a custodian. I learned more about humility and service to God than any seminary class could have ever taught me. It wasn't what I wanted to do long-term, but I knew if I was faithful, God would expand my horizon. As I would vacuum the sanctuary carpet and clean bathrooms, I learned to worship God through prayer and music. At the time, I was worried and in a hurry for the next place that God wanted me to be. But I learned then that God wasn't as concerned with *where* as he was concerned with *what* he wanted to do.

What I found out during those times allowed me to exercise faith in the future. If you want to use your faith muscle in taking risks, you have to be obedient to the calling in front of you. In my opinion, it takes more courage to wait for God's timing than to try to make things happen on your own. Even after we take an initial step, the next step might not be meant to follow immediately behind. You may have to wait.

Life is composed of seasons and transitions, especially spiritually. We often experience Lent as a "land between," a desert we cross before reaching the mountaintop or the Promised Land.[4]

Often, we reach the land between unexpectedly, almost like a sudden explosion or a natural disaster. This type of experience doesn't discriminate by age, gender, or race. It affects all of humanity. It can happen in a second, with a single sentence.

"We are downsizing, and your position is being eliminated."

"There's been an accident. How soon can you get to the hospital?"

"I don't love you anymore and want a divorce."

"I'm sorry, but your daughter has leukemia."

"The only way forward is going to be through bankruptcy."

Other times, we enter the land between by way of a seemingly never-ending series of "terrible, horrible, no good, very bad days." Though the circumstances may not individually be catastrophic, we find ourselves beaten up, exhausted, and discouraged through the cumulative effect.

Whether it happens suddenly or gradually, our faith is tested during these times when our life takes a different course than expected. The land between can be discouraging, frustrating, and draining as we struggle with the temptation to give up hope. However, the land between doesn't have to be a black hole. On the contrary, it can be an opportunity to more deeply experience and express gratitude for God's enduring blessings and provision.

Here are some things to remember if you find yourself in the land between.

1. **God will provide for you.** The children of Israel were taken care of with manna that fell from the sky to feed their physical bodies, and water from a rock to quench their thirst. It happened not when they wanted it, but when they were about to give up. Likewise, God will provide for you in the dark and desert times. Don't be surprised when you may sense an extra measure of his power and grace.

2. **God's presence will minister to you.** When we are going through the land between, the first temptation is to give up reading Scripture, give up our prayer life, and withdraw from God. But it's during the dry seasons that God will make us stronger. When Jesus went through his temptation in the desert, he practiced being in his Father's presence by quoting Scripture.

3. **God is preparing you.** Jesus went through the desert as a precursor to his season of public ministry—and he sought and found God's presence in both seasons. The in-between is preparation and a training ground

for a new season filled with opportunities, growth, and challenges around the corner. It's not something you are going through for the heck of it. It's something you will share with others. It brings God's strength into our human weakness and healing and wholeness where we have been empty and broken.

Our culture detests waiting.

Why won't our house sell?

How long do I have to wait for this difficult person to change?

When will I hear back about the job opportunity?

Why is this line so long?

When will I meet Ms. or Mr. Right?

We have become a culture of microwave popcorn and drive-thru fast food. We want to microwave all our situations, including our spirituality. The reality is that the latest book by a megachurch pastor or a spirituality conference isn't automatically going to draw you closer to God or turn your calling into reality. So what do we do when we're in life's waiting room?

Waiting doesn't mean sitting on your hands while the uncertainty sucks the life out of you. Here are a few practices to try the next time you're on hold.

1. **Active waiting.** Waiting doesn't mean giving up, clocking out, or distracting ourselves from the things we're waiting for. While you wait, you don't

have to sit still with your hands on your lap. Keep knocking on doors; just don't knock doors down out of impatience. Live your life, but don't forge ahead without God; check in with God about the direction you're going in.

2. **Waiting as a spiritual discipline.** We live in hope for what is to come while taking in the presence of God in the moment. Psalm 46:10 says, "Be still, and know that I am God!" Don't fight the waiting. Live in the waiting and embrace it as a way to draw closer to God.

3. **Expectant waiting.** The word *wait* means "to expect" or "to look for." God will show up when we wait expectantly. Jesus appeared to his disciples after the Resurrection. Paul and Silas were rescued from their prison cell with an earthquake. Live in anticipation of what might happen. It matters what we do in the waiting. It matters what God teaches us and shows us while we're waiting. But we have to look for God's movement and expect it in order to learn and see.

Now, let's take a look at the stories of Angie, Tim, Rudy, Jordan, Jason, Tom and Sandy, Chandi and Jamel, and Callie to understand what pushing away from shore— or walking into the land between—meant in their lives.

Angie Pushes Away from Shore

Angie was alone in the bathroom of her Nashville apartment, stuck in an addiction to cocaine. She lay on the floor depressed and started to reflect on her life and the choices she had made, when she heard the small, still voice of God. He said, "You are going to be OK." God was inviting Angie back into relationship. Angie started on the journey to recovery trusting God's voice. Little did she know what God had in store for her.

———

I was called to ministry. In my heart and mind I was under the conviction that the call was a call to prepare. But I didn't know: Do I go to seminary, not go to seminary? I had to go back and finish my bachelors. I had some unfinished work that needed to be done first, so it was difficult to discern how that was supposed to go.

———

Tim Pushes Away from Shore

After a broken marriage and a losing battle with alcohol, Tim decided enough was enough. Tim walked into Ginghamsburg Church during a packed Christmas Eve service. He didn't know this single decision was going to change his entire life's course.

I didn't grow up in church and knew little about Christianity, but that night the Good News was presented to me in a powerful way. That evening I made a commitment to follow Jesus. I quit drinking and got immersed in the daily life of the church in service opportunities, mission trips, Bible studies, and even helped start a biker ministry called Broken Chains.

I suffered a heart attack, which left me devastated and wondering what I had done wrong. I learned I had a genetic defect that predisposed me to heart issues. It didn't stop me from doing what I loved to do. As an engineer by day, I continued to serve at church whenever I got a free moment. One day as I was picking up my medication from the local pharmacy, I noticed the pharmacist. After a few more visits, I worked up the courage to ask her out after noticing she didn't have a wedding ring on her finger. After a few dates, Donna and I were inseparable, and we eventually fell in love and got married.

Everything seemed to be working out, but I had two more heart attacks that forced me to retire. "How could God allow this to happen?" I asked myself. Discouraged and not being able to work did a number on my pride.

Rudy Pushes Away from Shore

Rudy and his wife, Juanita, pastor St. John's United Methodist Church in Houston, Texas. They started the church in 1992 with only nine members. Twenty-five years later, the church has just over 9,000 members, and 30 percent of those members were previously homeless. Rudy and Juanita minister to a diverse congregation with people from all walks of life.

Rudy recently encountered some disillusionment with the church and its culture. He pastored St. John's during the megachurch boom. He thought about retiring but didn't feel released by God. While Rudy waited in a period of discernment, he began to sense that his ministry was going in a different direction.

As Rudy is approaching the twilight of his vocational ministry as pastor of St. John's, he has decided once again to push away from shore.

It was about seven years ago when I really started to wake up to the fact that my season would ultimately shift in pastoral ministry. My therapist challenged me to ask this question: What did I want my life to say when I was no longer here to articulate it myself? And that was the turning point. After spending some time thinking about what I wanted my life to say, it dawned on me that I wanted to help young people realize their dream. There was a condition: as long as that

*dream not only helped them, but helped someone
else that they didn't know.*

Jordan Pushes Away from Shore

I first met Jordan when she arrived in Dayton, Ohio, as a
first-year seminary student at United Theological Seminary.
Jordan never thought she would be going to seminary,
especially Dayton of all places. Who in their right mind
would want to leave the warm weather of sunny Florida to
face the unpredictable weather of Dayton? It was God's call
where Jordan left her comfortable shore to go into an area
that was foreign to her.

---

*Being from Florida and being called up to
Dayton, Ohio, was a way I pushed away from
shore. I had no idea what I was getting into,
not having any family or connections here. All
I knew about was the seminary and the peace
of God.*

Jason Pushes Away from Shore

In some ways, Jason's story is similar to Rudy's. Called
into ministry, he has experienced not one, but two dis-
tinct periods of "pushing away from shore" and awaiting
God's call.

31

I always wanted to be an artist. Then, in junior high or high school, I went on a Chrysalis weekend (which is the youth version of an Emmaus Walk). It was there that I heard and felt God calling me to ministry. This was confusing to me; I had never heard of an artist in ministry. So I struggled with that for a while.

I graduated from high school and was playing in a band. A lot of the guys in the band went to Ginghamsburg Church in Tipp City, Ohio. I was going to an art school with a big commercial arts program. That summer, I got a position at the church I had grown up in. It was an internship, and I had to turn down my regular job at the local park system, which actually paid decent money. To make up for the loss of income, I thought I'd do some freelance art. A band member mentioned I should try to do some work at Ginghamsburg. At the time I thought, "What church knows anything about graphic design?" Without telling me, the band member set up an interview at Ginghamsburg and told me to show up the next morning with my portfolio.

I showed up, shared my portfolio, and was given a couple projects to work on. I was supposed to design a preschool logo and brochure *for children's ministry. I didn't even have a computer at the time, so they said I could come use their computers any time I wanted. While I was working on my original project, the person in charge of media ministry came down and asked whether I could make a graphic of a door for worship that weekend. I did, and they used it as a graphic. I got invited to the next staff meeting, and the lead pastor went crazy about the graphic. I remember thinking, "This is kinda cool. I could work for a place like this."*

After that, I started getting all these requests for various graphics. I still wasn't getting paid, and I didn't have time to complete the original projects I'd been assigned.

I was enjoying the work and learning more all the time but was still uncertain what the future would bring.

Tom and Sandy Push Away from Shore

We have to go back to the late '90s for our pushing away from shore. We were thinking about retirement at that time, and our kids had all gotten married and left the house. We had a great big farmhouse the two of us were rattling around in with more than an acre of grass to mow. And I'm saying to Sandy, "I'm not doing this house in my retirement. This is not gonna happen." So we started thinking, "Well, what does the Lord have for us to do? How can we get rid of this place and be available to God?" We had no idea that a ministry in China was on the horizon. So we're thinking about downsizing and saving money.

We had people telling us, "You've got this big farmhouse, you need to start a B&B. You need to keep this as your retirement investment." But we sensed God saying, "Push away from what the rest of the world is doing and recommending, and follow me." So we did. We got rid of the big farmhouse and moved into the little three-room apartment. That was quite a move; it took two years to do it, just to get rid of everything and do some remodeling and fixing to get into the apartment.

Making plans ahead of time to be available to the Lord, whether that's tomorrow or two years away, is pushing away. It's also pushing away from what the rest of the world thinks is a good idea to find God's perfect plan. We weren't prepared for the blessing we were about to receive just by pushing away.

We got free from the tyranny of stuff. When we moved to the one-bedroom apartment, we felt like the whole world was lifted off our shoulders. The world's standard of having all this stuff was gone, and we were free.

Chandi and Jamel Push Away from Shore

Chandi knew she wanted a different life than the one she had grown up in. Drugs, addiction, and destructive behavior were her norm. This was modeled for her from a young age. As a young newlywed, Chandi realized she carried some baggage into the marriage, and so did her husband Jamel. Jamel had become comfortable with promiscuity, and it didn't stop after marriage. Rather than leave the marriage or confront the issues, Chandi's low self-esteem kept her in dysfunction. While inebriated one night, which was how she numbed her pain, she realized how miserable she was and knew she had had enough. Chandi called out to God. Chandi pushed away from shore and made the decision to turn her life around along with her marriage. How she would do so remained to be seen. She knew she could work on her self-esteem and other issues, but how could she help Jamel? Chandi's decision to push away from shore initiated the couple's decision to begin counseling, which in turn opened the door to transparency and hope.

Callie Pushes Away from Shore

Unlike some of the other individuals whose stories we have begun looking into, Callie's "pushing away from shore" moment began with a decision that was not her own: her husband's—that is, *my*—decision to move churches (and states) to a place neither of us had lived and that would uproot her from her long-term job. Let's take a closer look.

In January 2014, Roz and I accepted God's call to move to Dayton, Ohio, so that Roz could accept a position as Executive Church Pastor of New Congregational Development at Ginghamsburg Church. We were leaving family, friends, jobs we loved, our church, our home, and the community we'd lived in since before we were married. But God had called, so we said yes. The question for me was, what would I be doing for employment? I explored multiple possibilities and had a couple job offers, including one to work for United Theological Seminary and one to continue working for National Christian Foundation Kentucky, where I had worked the previous six years, but to do so remotely and begin to develop new relationships for the organization in the Dayton area.

Callie left everything she had known for many years to go into uncharted waters. Though she was excited about following God's call, it came with a bit of fear and trepidation. As a self-proclaimed planner, Callie likes to have everything laid out. Leaving the predictable and guaranteed stability of a job she loved was not easy. However, she knew that God was going to honor her obedience as she pushed away from shore.

Chapter One Study Questions

1. What would it look like for you to treat each new day like you are "pushing away from shore?"
2. How can you expectantly await God's adventure in your life?
3. Has God ever given you an instruction that seems to mean "just wait and see"? How have you coped with the uncertainty of what lies ahead?
4. Has God ever felt too far away when you are awaiting his guidance? How might you feel closer to God while you wait?
5. Have you identified who else has "pushed off from shore" with you and your relationship with them? How can they help or hinder your trust in God while you await his call?

Chapter Two
Getting Spooked

Fear doesn't shut you down; it wakes you up.
                    —VERONICA ROTH

Without fear there cannot be courage.
                    —CHRISTOPHER PAOLINI

Shortly before dawn Jesus went out to them, walking on the lake. When the disciples saw him walking on the lake, they were terrified. "It's a ghost," they said, and cried out in fear.
                    —MATTHEW 14:25–26

When Jesus appeared, looking like a ghost on the water, it was in the wee hours of the night. Some scholars suggest it was between three and six in the morning.[1] The disciples were terrified at what they saw and heard—paralyzed with fear.

Some people live in almost constant fear because of their past hurts, hang-ups, and experiences that have altered their perspective. They live in fear not only by reliving what has already happened to them, but also by continuing to consider everything bad that *might* happen to them in the future.

Of course, nearly all of us, to one degree or another, have been crippled by fear at some point in our life, whether for only a moment or for an entire season; therefore, we can all sympathize, at least in part, with those who over-focus on fears. Moreover, during times of intense stress and fear—whether facing a mountain lion or just having learned of the death of a loved one—a portion of our nervous system known as the vagus nerve can signal our body not to "fight or flight," but rather to "freeze or faint." Indeed, the idea of being paralyzed with fear is not purely metaphorical thanks to the vagus nerve. No wonder, then, that even when faced with what could have become a divine calling for any of them, nearly all of the disciples failed to get out of the boat.

A lot of what we face in life is a matter of perspective. Renowned NCAA football coach Urban Meyer challenges his players by saying that "events plus response equals outcome."[2] We cannot control most of the events that happen to us in life. We can't control how we end up in the boat, even if we don't want to be in it. We can't control what has happened to us in the past or the cards we've been dealt. But we *can* control our responses. Our responses are a matter of perspective. If we constantly surround ourselves with negativity and people who view their lives as half empty, that negativity will rub off on us.

We always have a choice of how to respond when we are in the boat. Are we going to respond with fear or faith? Inactivity or movement? Negativity or positivity? I'm not suggesting looking at every situation with rose-colored glasses and our head in the clouds, but I do make a practice of surrounding myself with people of faith so that I may be sharpened even more in faith when I'm in "the fire." Moreover, our response to a trying and chaotic situation can help change the outcome.

For reasons we may never understand, Peter was the type of person who had a different perspective. Even after pushing off from shore, Peter knew to expect adventure following Jesus. Sitting in a boat amid high waves and darkness, he knew he would not always understand Jesus' next plans or goals, yet he trusted enough to do what Jesus asked of him. Some would mistake his faith for foolishness; perhaps the other disciples did at that very moment. One question we may wonder about is whether Peter was ever as terrified as the other disciples. If not, what made him so different such that, as soon as Jesus called to them, Peter reacted quickly without any indication of fear? While we don't know exactly what raced through Peter's mind in those moments, a part of the difference between Peter's response and the rest of the disciples' responses was a difference in perspective. Peter shaped the outcome of his situation by having a different perspective. He chose to get out of the boat. Peter's perspective led to action and not giving in to the inactivity like the rest of the disciples.

Does perception have to be reality? When I tell people I left Lexington, Kentucky, to move to Trotwood, Ohio (a suburb of Dayton), they do a double take. A few years back, Dayton was one of the top ten fastest dying cities in America. Fortunately, it is coming back economically, but Trotwood is still feeling the effects of decline. Walmart, Target, Applebee's, and numerous other businesses have closed their doors in Trotwood. The vacant old restaurant buildings, home foreclosures, and empty commercial space are what people notice at first glance. Trotwood was once the destination for people from surrounding parts of Ohio because it was thriving and even had the first shopping mall in the area. But that is no longer the case. Because of the economic decline, the perception of Trotwood has been that it is crime-ridden and that the people of Trotwood are troubled. This couldn't be farther from the truth. The people of Trotwood are resilient and tight-knit, and they look out for one another.

The apostle Paul said in 2 Corinthians 5:16, "From now on, therefore, we regard no one according to the flesh. Even though we once regarded Christ according to the flesh, we regard him thus no longer." When we come to know Jesus, we no longer look at people or places the same way, through the eyes of the flesh; we no longer look at what they've done in the past, or who they are presently. Instead, when we put on the mind of Christ and look through the eyes of faith, we see what is possible. A new perception, through the eyes of faith, can be a reality that God desires as we pray for God's kingdom to break through the worldly kingdoms on earth. In Trotwood, I don't see a dead and forgotten place, but one where revival can happen and spill over to the city of Dayton.

Think back to the disciples. Amid their terror, what they likely first perceived when Jesus spoke was a ghost speaking. Interestingly, in verse 27 Jesus gives the command, "Take courage." It wasn't a suggestion or thought but a command. Peter, on the other hand, likely didn't see a ghost but may have already recognized Jesus—or, at the least, recognized his voice when he spoke. Peter took it seriously as he heard the voice of Jesus. It was a voice that was familiar to him because it was one he heard in the context of relationship. Too often we listen to the wrong voices around us.

I grew up in a loving family. My parents emigrated from Sicily to western New York. They both had the equivalent of a middle school education. My family didn't prioritize education. All they cared about was that I passed to the next grade and tried to behave myself. When I entered high school, I started thinking about my future. My parents didn't have the money to send me to college, and I didn't want to attend a local community college because I knew I had to break ties with some friendships that were dragging me down. When I talked to my parents about leaving my hometown, I was met with resistance. In a Sicilian family, sons and daughters are supposed to stay in the household until they get married, and then they live in the same hometown or village to take care of aging parents. Yet I knew I needed to go to college.

Stepping out of that boat, I was admitted into a small Christian liberal arts school of about 1,200 students. It saved my life in more ways than one, based on the direction I was heading. My friends were using and selling drugs, gambling, and getting into other trouble. I needed to get out of my environment. I needed to leave the boat and be the first one in my family to graduate from college. I would have never done so if I gave into fear and peer pressure, even when it came from the people who cared about me the most.

Those we surround ourselves with and listen to can influence our perspective. The apostle Paul says in Romans 12:2, "Do not conform to the pattern of this world, but be transformed by the renewing of your mind. Then you will be able to test and approve what God's will is—his good, pleasing and perfect will."

The renewing of the mind is the way we gain perspective with the eyes of faith. What we think can shape what we see. The renewal of our mind is patterning ourselves not after someone else, but after the mind of Jesus, which will help us discern God's call and will for our lives.

Angie Is Spooked

Coming out of addiction—a life of being high probably 75 percent of my day—was terrifying. As I started to do the work and NA groups and live sober, everything was scary. Going to church and encountering the Holy Spirit, there were negative spirits that [were leaving me], and I was being renewed in my spirit. Of course, this is a great thing. But it was all new. I was not accustomed to operating in a spiritual way, so it was terrifying.

Chandi and Jamel Are Spooked

There were times on the journey when fear set in for Chandi and Jamel, especially as they began to dig into their own issues. They had to work on themselves and their marriage by discovering a new way of life. They never thought that the road to healing would lead them to do relationship conferences, talk shows, and speaking on a national platform about their own hurts and hang-ups. As they took their private issues and made them public, they were afraid whether people would show up and listen to them. If people did show up, would they face judgment and ridicule? Marital issues and sex are not often discussed in public, let alone in a church setting. As God began to open the doors, Chandi and Jamel took the steps in faith.

As Jamel began to make life changes, he made himself a T-shirt to remind him of being a one-woman guy. The shirt said, "God Body," and the verse from 1 Corinthians about our bodies being the temple of the Holy Spirit was printed underneath. Jamel viewed this shirt as his armor. It was a visible reminder of an internal struggle he faced. At first, he was afraid of people asking him about the shirt. He didn't want to share the shirt's backstory. But as he did, something surprising took place. Others wanted the shirt too. Jamel has been able to sell approximately 1,000 God Body T-shirts, hoodies, and other apparel a year. Jamel's internal fear became a source of freedom to others as he told his story.

Chapter Two Study Questions

1. Think back to your past. Name a time when you gave in to fear, even though part of you knew you should have been looking for hope.
2. Why do you think it is so easy to feel paralyzed by fear instead of being ready to step out in faith when God calls?

3. What voices in your life do you most frequently listen to? Are they more likely to reaffirm your fears and reinforce a "half-empty" mentality or to encourage you in your faith and help you listen to God's call?

4. In light of your reflections, what changes do you need to make in terms of voices you are listening to or your own personal attitude toward your circumstances?

Chapter Three
Identifying the Boat

Coming out of your comfort zone is tough in the beginning, chaotic in the middle, and awesome in the end . . . because in the end, it shows you a whole new world.

—MANOJ ARORA

But Jesus immediately said to them: "Take courage! It is I. Don't be afraid." "Lord, if it's you," Peter replied, "tell me to come to you on the water." "Come," he said. Then Peter got down out of the boat, walked on the water and came toward Jesus.

—MATTHEW 14:27–29

After Jesus identified himself, Peter decided to literally walk his faith. Logic would have told him that, regardless of the shape his particular boat was in, it was better to be in any boat than out of it in a storm, attempting to walk on water! This is certainly what logic told the other disciples aboard. Yet Peter decided he would leave the boat, enter the storm, and experience (even if fleetingly in this case) the sustaining power of Jesus.

What boat is God calling you out of? What earthly security blanket do you need to leave behind to experience adventure? What fears are clenching your attention, blocking you from stepping out of the boat to follow Christ? In our search for the adventure God calls us to, we must begin by identifying the boat we're in. Identifying our own boat and the reasons we're clinging to it can release us to hear and follow God's call. Maybe it's a toxic relationship, a lifestyle, an addiction, a coping mechanism, or some other crutch we must put aside.

Often, these "boats" of life are like unreliable dinghies keeping us mere inches from the ravages of life's seas. Yet at times, we experience success that can also be a boat— albeit, one more like a luxury yacht we own and command. Like failure, success—especially when it is a known quantity—is cozy. In success, we might be earning more money than ever before, living in our dream home, or planning our happy future with the person of our dreams. When we experience success, we feel safe, cared for, and that our work or our path has been validated. Success can also bring feelings of insulation, pride, self-worth, and self-reliance, all of which are dangerous and destructive apart from God.

We can see this in the parable of the rich young man, that our boat may be our wealth, our home, or even our friends and family. From Matthew 19:16–25:

Just then a man came up to Jesus and asked, "Teacher, what good thing must I do to get eternal life?"

"Why do you ask me about what is good?" Jesus replied. "There is only One who is good. If you want to enter life, keep the commandments." . . .

"All these I have kept," the young man said. "What do I still lack?"

Jesus answered, "If you want to be perfect, go, sell your possessions and give to the poor, and you will have treasure in heaven. Then come, follow me."

When the young man heard this, he went away sad, because he had great wealth.

Then Jesus said to his disciples, "Truly I tell you, it is hard for someone who is rich to enter the kingdom of heaven.

Of course, Jesus is not saying that in order to truly follow him, everyone must give up all wealth and turn their backs on friends, family, and spouses. He is warning us, however, not to cling to each of these things above God for our comfort, strength, and refuge. He is also telling us that there may be times when, in order to follow his commands, we will need to leave comforts behind or get out of the boat.

We can find an excellent example of identifying a boat in the life of bestselling author and former megachurch pastor Francis Chan. Chan started Cornerstone Church in his living room, and by 2010, the church had grown to 5,000 in attendance and was still growing. So why in the world would Chan leave the megachurch he founded? Many pastors spend their whole ministry career trying to build their church. Given that the average size of a church in America is around one hundred people in attendance, Chan's ministry could be seen as highly successful. God had used Chan to do something remarkable, but Chan wasn't fulfilled by his newly found "celebrity status" as a megachurch pastor.

Chan recently spoke to another organization that has experienced growth and success—Facebook. Revealing his heart, Chan shared that he had become comfortable at Cornerstone Church and had found false fulfillment in it. Chan admitted his pride by saying, "Everything you (God) said you hated, that's me right now. I gotta get out of here. I'm losing my soul."[1] Chan lost himself in the process of taking part in something that was growing. He lost the passion he had found as a Christian during his high school years.

Chan shocked the evangelical world when he resigned from Cornerstone Church. Rather than taking a role at a larger church or becoming a CEO of a Christian organization, Chan pursued a call from God that he couldn't shake. This meant getting back to the root of what he wanted to do as a pastor: equipping other men and women to be the church. In 2013, Chan started the We Are Church planting network as a collection of house churches. Each church meets in a home and has two pastors overseeing it. The pastors are unpaid. Tithes and offerings are collected at the gathering, but all of it goes to missions and outreach. Currently, the network is comprised of fourteen or fifteen house churches with about thirty unpaid pastors.[2] There is zero overhead, and people are joining in because they want to be part of an authentic Christian community that feels like a family. Chan himself doesn't take a salary. He made a million dollars from his book *Crazy Love* and signed it all over to a charitable trust, designated to other organizations. Chan is more fulfilled now than ever before. He doesn't have to preach weekly in front of the masses because he has equipped others to do the preaching and teaching in the house churches. We Are Church flies in the face of cult personalities and the attractional model; instead, it's simple.[3]

Francis Chan stepped out of the boat to follow God's next call for him even when other people didn't understand. Most people in Chan's position would not have left Cornerstone Church and a position as a megachurch pastor.

Chan felt an unrest and knew he had to take action—even if that meant leaving behind what God had used him to build in the first place. In his day, Jesus could have built the biggest megachurch. Instead, he spent 80 percent of his time investing in twelve people. These men weren't the smartest, but they were willing to follow Jesus. Many crowds gathered to hear Jesus' teaching and witness the miracles. But at the end of the day, Jesus challenged them, and they didn't want to follow him. Jesus could have made the challenges he issued in his teaching easier, more seeker friendly, and attractional. Jesus' goal was to build disciples, not masses. At the end of Jesus' earthly ministry, people could have said he was a failure or a one-hit wonder. Yet it was the twelve disciples who received the Holy Spirit and who grew the church to what it is today.

Angie's Boat

A message that I still remember when I first came back to Christ and the church is that God said get out of the boat. He challenges us to get out of our comfort zone and serve: teach Sunday school or lead the community and witness to people. He challenges us to do more than just come in and sit on the pews. I needed to be challenged. If life was comfortable and seemed to be working, I was OK just sitting in the pews. But when I'm challenged, I move forward and seek different experiences. You've got to try to put your toes in the water.

Tim's Boat

Tim has stepped out of many boats in the last ten to twenty years, but he describes one boat that he has to leave on a daily basis.

For me it's always the same. It's part of my past. It's not as bad today, but it's still there. I'm not good enough. There's a fear of failure. Fear of not being good enough, not smart enough because I didn't go to college. I think there's more of the "I'm not smart enough, not good enough" than even the fear of failure. You know how life is; it can make you feel this way too. How you were treated by your parents can contribute.[4]

Rudy's Boat

Four years ago, I met this young barista who was probably the most knowledgeable coffee person I had ever met. He really, really loved coffee. And this guy really convinced me that we could do a coffee shop together. So we started working on it.

I had no idea how much it would cost to really start a coffee shop. I had no idea. I'm thinking, man, just a coffee maker, right? We started working on it, started hitting road-blocks. I started realizing it was going to take a whole lot more than just a simple missional shop to compete in this big coffee market. That's when I realized we were going to have to really make an investment into this shop.

Jordan's Boat

I was afraid to commit to a church because of the unknown. What gifts and talents did I have to offer in this church system that seems so amazing? I remember looking at this job description for a position at The Point and feeling totally inadequate. I literally just crumpled up the paper and threw it in the trash. I made a basket. I was looking at my own inexperience.

Jason's Boat

When I approached my boss with the issue of having so much work to do without pay, I was immediately given an internship at Ginghamsburg. Right from the start, I was putting in thirty-five to forty hours a week. At this same time, the church was doing a national search for an art director, flying candidates in from all over. I was told that the church wanted me to be interviewed too. They called me in the next day and told me they'd given me the position.

I was hired in January. I finished school, and the very next day was my first day on staff. In part because of the creative stuff we were doing in worship, the church began to experience rapid growth. CBS came to do an interview about our innovative approaches to worship. Our media and worship were getting national attention.

In the three years I was on staff, we had begun doing conferences on media and worship design. People came from across the country to learn from us. This was the time when I began to see Ginghamsburg as a boat God would be calling me out of.

The fact that Ginghamsburg appreciated the role of art and media in worship design, and the fact that I could see the positive consequences of its use, were very affirming and exciting for me. I had a lot of freedom to make artistic choices, try new things, and a decent budget to go along with that.

However, I got the sense there was some other cause God was calling me to, and I began to listen for that.

Tom and Sandy's Boat

We had in mind what we had thought our ministry was going to look like for several years. It turned out that wasn't what God had planned for us. So in one sense, getting out of the boat was leaving our own expectations behind. In another sense, after our trips to China to see family and with the understanding that God might be calling us to ministry there, getting out of the boat was realizing the extent to which we would be leaving a "normal" comfortable life, our native language, and our family and friends behind to venture into something almost completely unknown to us.

Chandi and Jamel's Boat

Chandi and Jamel's boat, as odd as it sounds, was their own misery. After years of misery and imprisonment, they had grown accustomed to it. They had to make the conscious choice to pursue wholeness and healing. They began to realize that the old adage, "you are only as sick as your secrets," was true. As they began attending worship together and as they became more transparent with each other, counselors, and wise friends, they were able to identify the boat they had been in and make progress toward leaving it behind. This was not an easy step for either of them. In fact, it was uncomfortable plenty of times. Chandi was ready to be transparent, but Jamel had a difficult time expressing himself because of his own indiscretion and worries about others' perceptions of him.

Callie's Boat

Callie had seen friends, mentors, and family members model what it meant to step out of the boat. She was comfortable in her work, but she had the sense something more was on the horizon.

I loved my job with National Christian Fellowship Kentucky, so it made sense to continue that in Dayton. It was fun and I was good at it. I was definitely comfortable there, and with changing everything else in life, sta-bility with work seemed a nice perk.

Chapter Three Study Questions

1. How do you prepare yourself for the next adventure God has planned for you?

2. Have you ever found yourself in a toxic "boat," using it as a crutch instead of leaning on God's plan for your life?

3. Have you ever been, or do you find yourself now, in a situation that feels just a little too comfortable? Too insulated from the world's problems? Too insulated from others whom God might call and equip you to help? Leaning on your own understanding and your own capabilities?

4. Do you prioritize safety, comfort, or predictability over the adventure God calls you to? How could you begin to shift your priorities, day by day?

5. Do you lean on certain people, hobbies, pleasures, or even your job for your main source of comfort and strength? Do you think God calls you to give anything up to better follow him, or are there other ways you can prioritize God over these comforts?

Chapter Four

Asking for God's Call

I believe there's a calling for all of us. I know that every human being has value and purpose. The real work of our lives is to become aware. And awakened. To answer the call.

—OPRAH WINFREY

"Lord, if it's you," Peter replied, "tell me to come to you on the water."

—MATTHEW 14:28

What did Peter do when he realized Jesus was walking on the water? Did he analyze the physics, question why Jesus was out there in the first place, consider what purpose this could achieve, or whether he personally was equipped to walk on water? Did he wonder why Jesus hadn't simply appeared in the boat or drawn the boat to the shore where

Jesus was instead of walking across the sea? In contrast, Peter simply asked Jesus to call him out on the water.

Consider Peter's motivations in asking Jesus to call him out on the water. Often when we think about God's call on our lives, we imagine a role we might play to evangelize, minister to, counsel, heal, or provide for others. While God does often call individuals to these roles, Peter was not asking for this type of call out on the boat. He was staring at Jesus standing on the water as if it were solid ground. He had already watched Jesus perform miracles to feed people earlier in the day. He was devoted to learning from and obeying Jesus. In the moment that Peter asks for Jesus' call, he simply wants to be nearer to him, to experience the miraculous nature and joy of Jesus' power working through him. He's not even asking in this moment to help someone else—though he likely gave the other disciples on the boat a sense of awe and adoration when they witnessed this scene!

Similarly, when we ask for God's call, we ought to remember that God doesn't call us to do anything he couldn't do without us. Asking for and accepting God's call is, first and foremost, about being in communion with the Holy Spirit, allowing God's work to be done through us for the sake of our own redemption and the redemption of others.

Jesus doesn't need us to ask for his call. And sometimes, Jesus doesn't wait for us to ask for his call. But when we do ask for God's call, we alert ourselves and prepare ourselves for the answer we might receive.

First, by asking for God's call, we acknowledge within ourselves the desire to hear God's call. We expectantly await that God will lead us when it's needed. It is an acknowledgment of our faith that God will respond, that God knows the plans he has for us, and that God will reveal those plans in his perfect time. We cultivate a desire for God to work through us, to be close to God and others in this way.

Second, by asking for God's call, we begin to activate our willingness to respond to and obey God's call. We have the chance to prepare our hearts to listen, hear, and follow. We may begin to discern the purpose of the skills (spiritual or otherwise) with which God has equipped us, or the circumstances for which he has equipped us.

In fact, asking is an active test of our own trust. Peter wanted to find out for himself whether he *could* walk on the water, yet he was prepared to believe that he could. He wanted to find out for himself whether Jesus *would* give him the power to walk on the water, yet he was prepared to believe that he would.

Asking for God's call is asking for something greater than ourselves, something we can't accomplish on our own. For Peter, this was walking on the water. Later for Peter, this was to be building the church. Talk about a task Peter couldn't accomplish on his own! Each of us must ask for God's call, preparing to step into God's adventure for us.

Angie Asks for God's Call

While Angie was in the boat, waiting to discern what God's call to ministry looked like for her, she cultivated a deep prayer life.

I started an intercessory prayer ministry at the church. We prayed for the church, and the people who would come, and for the service each Sunday. Over the course of four or five months, I received the call. This was serious, deep prayer time—not for myself, but for the ministry and for others to come to Christ and be saved. In that deep prayer life, I heard the call.

Tim Asks for God's Call

I left work after the heart attacks, and as a man, my whole life has revolved around what I do at work. And I look back on that twenty years of work now; that's something you do and you do it well and provide for your family. But God didn't give me a gift to go to work at Emerson for twenty years. He gave me a gift to be a pastor and care for and love others and tell others about Christ. Maybe I had to "retire" to figure out what God's calling actually was.

Rudy Asks for God's Call

Hanging out in coffee shops has always been a pastime for Rudy. Despite pastoring a large congregation, Rudy found he was more easily able to strike up spiritual conversations—without catching people off guard as "the pastor"—in the informality and comfort of a coffee shop. Between this and regular spiritual retreats to seek God's will, Rudy realized that a God-centered coffee shop might be exactly what God was calling him to.

Jordan Asks for God's Call

Then I was back in seminary and had to commit to a site placement. I asked the formation leader whether there were any openings. I'm a bridge and outreach leader. Bridge from the community to the life of the church.

Jason Asks for God's Call

About three years into my position at Ginghamsburg, my sometimes-boss, sometimes-colleague and I had the chance to collaborate on some projects outside of our Ginghamsburg relationship. We worked on some videos and marketing projects together, and we both really enjoyed the experience. We both started thinking about how we could use what we had learned in the past few years to help other small- and medium-sized churches, churches like the one I'd grown up in, use more innovative approaches to their own worship design. Len and I started dreaming together about what this would look like. We were excited, but we saw it as a pipe dream. How could we possibly get people to sign up for this? What would the business aspects look like?

Tom and Sandy Ask for God's Call

We really thought maybe the Lord had a ministry to Muslim people in mind. Tom had worked with some Muslims. We were praying for a ministry to Muslims, assuming that would be somewhere here in the US, knowing that we're not really welcome in many Muslim countries.

Chandi and Jamel Ask for God's Call

Chandi and Jamel didn't ask for God's call through traditional prayer and quiet time. Instead, they actually said a prayer of desperation for God to rescue their marriage and lives. They were asking for a life change. As God began providing answers, he also began calling Chandi and Jamel deeper than they initially realized. It became their deep desire to see people gain freedom and healing in their lives. They continued to ask for God's call by asking for their own healing as they went to counseling, church, and began to read Scripture.

Callie Asks for God's Call

I was praying and listening for God's will, journaling, and talking with trusted friends and family. But for me, one of the most significant ways I hear from the Lord is through spiritual direction. For those who have never done spiritual direction, it resembles counseling in some ways, sharing what's going on with a trained individual who listens and asks you questions as you seek to discern what to do. But it goes deeper to praying through Scripture and listening to God speak in your heart. Those are things that can be done alone, but in the context of spiritual direction, you have someone affirming what is of God, questioning and probing deeper when you are on the edge of discovery, and praying for you throughout.

Anytime I'm going through a season of transition, I intentionally make it a priority to meet with a spiritual director.

———————

Chapter Four Study Questions

1. Have you ever felt certain that God was working through you to reach others? What did this feel like? How did you know?
2. Are you ready for the adventure that will result from asking for God's call?
3. Have you asked God to call you? When you ask God for his call, do you ask believing that you will receive or are you fearful that God will not respond—or that he will respond in a way you do not like?

Chapter Five

Hearing the Call

Our failure to hear His voice when we want
to is due to the fact that we do not in general
want to hear it, that we want it only when we
think we need it.

—DALLAS WILLARD

"Come," he said.

—MATTHEW 14:29A

Peter had spent months with Jesus at this time and was accustomed to listening to Jesus and hearing his truths. Therefore, all it took from Jesus was one simple, direct word to Peter: "Come."

Yet if we aren't in the habit of hearing God speak to us, and if we aren't waiting readily for his leading, how easy might it be for us to miss God's call? Sometimes we can look back and see that God was calling us at different times along the path when we weren't prepared or practiced enough to hear.

God generally does not speak to us in giant ways but in small ways. When we are waiting for some kind of spectacular experience to get our attention, we are usually going to be disappointed. God rarely yells; God whispers.[1] When we are in a crowded room and someone speaks softly, we have to lean in to hear what they have to say. Are you leaning in today to hear what Jesus has to say to you?

John Wesley, the founder of Methodism, believed that God's calling comes in two parts. The first is an *inner* call, confirmed through the gifts and graces for ministry that a person possesses. The second is an *outward* call, which comes through the church.[2] Sometimes the church and an individual's network of friends and mentors see something in a person that he or she has never considered. Others call it out, and when we take the step of operating in these gifts, we feel alive.

Some folks only look for an inward call—think *American Idol.* We've all watched the individuals who, without a musical bone in their bodies, show up to audition. Certainly no one has told these participants that they are great singers prior to their decision to audition; it's almost as if it they are living in their own world. They see themselves completely differently than others see them, including their friends and family. They might be commended for pursuing their dream, but because their gifts don't match up with those of Kelly Clarkson, they will not be living into their own God-given adventure.

Others focus only on an outward call. A friend, teacher, pastor, or family member suggests a role or an opportunity they think would be perfect for an individual. Out of impatience ("This must be the call since I haven't heard anything else"), or a sense of obligation ("Well, my pastor thinks I should do this, so I guess I should"), or pride ("What an honor that I'm being asked to do this"), or maybe just out of a lack of something better to do, the individual gets carried away by a suggestion that they had no inward calling to. Can you relate?

Jerry Herships spent a better part of two decades in entertainment as a comedian and was surprised when his pastor told him he thought Herships had a call to ministry. (Did I mention that Jerry was also a bartender for ten years?) When God called him into seminary and ministry, he was forty years old. Jerry didn't know how he was going to fit in a normal church culture until he realized that church doesn't just happen in a certain room at a certain hour of the week; church can happen anywhere at any time. After seminary, Herships's call grew louder, to the point where he couldn't shake it. The call was to start a United Methodist Church called After Hours that meets—of all places—in a bar. Herships has gone right to the people and has expanded After Hours to multiple sites where God has used his experience as a comedian and bartender to stand in front of crowds and share his faith.

"I used to be a comedian, an emcee, and a host," Herships says. "That's still what I am. I host these 'happy hours' for God."[3] The most pushback Herships receives is not from his new guests, but rather from those who have been in church for a while because they don't understand or agree with the concept. That has not stopped or discouraged Herships from answering God's call. What's important is that Jerry took the first step and left his familiar world, not knowing at the time that God was going to call him back to the place he left in order to minister to those who otherwise would have been left behind.

When God calls us to do something—whether it is a lifelong mission or a next-step assignment—we will experience inward and outward confirmation. Sure, there will be critics along the way with ready criticism and discouragement, but it's the call that carries us through.

Angie Hears God's Call

Angie not only heard God while in the depths of her addiction, but she also heard a powerful call to ministry.

I had a midnight encounter. One night, the ceiling opened up. The heavens opened up. There was an illumination. God sat on the edge of the bed and talked, just casually talked to me. I have no idea how long it lasted, but it was for a period of time. I felt peaceful and comforted, safe. I was engaged. I thought, "This is the opportunity of a lifetime! I have the chance to ask God anything I want." He answered my questions, until I got to one that had been bothering me. I had asked, "What about the men?" I was in Nashville, and there was a major resistance to women being in ministry. The revelation ended then. I woke up in the morning and knew I had gotten a call.

At the time, I didn't have enough insight to know God was saying, "You need to do this in faith. You need to go trusting that I called you and not knowing ahead of time that certain segments of the population will accept you." I realized later that by not answering my last question, this was what God was telling me.

―――――

Tim Hears God's Call

For Tim, the biggest part of hearing God's call is being willing to say yes to what others are asking of him. Whether it's temporary service opportunities, just one person in need, starting an entire ministry, or becoming a pastor, Tim says yes and sees God's call in hindsight. Rides to Work provides transportation to people who need to get to their place of employment as well as to drug addiction counseling and doctors' appointments.

Folks in shelters can get a ride for free, and eventually, the cost is one dollar one-way. After ninety days, it's two dollars one-way. In 2016, Tim and his two other drivers gave over 5,000 rides to 163 individuals.

———————

I look back to the past, and things were leading up to it. I was in biker ministry for ten years. That's part of my call, but it's not the whole picture. Everything I've done has been on-the-job training. When God calls in my life, it looks like this. It looks like something that doesn't make sense. Somebody calls out of the blue, like the next-door neighbor comes and asks, "Hey, do you want to go teach Bible study at the jail?" Well, first of all, I don't know anything about jail. Second, I'm not a Bible study teacher. But just say yes. For me, it's saying yes to Jesus. Because I know that's my calling when I don't understand. If I understand something, it's probably something dumb that I've made up. It's probably not God. But all these visits to the jail made me realize, "I'm an evangelist; this guy's a Bible study teacher. We're powerful together." Then I started seeing the pieces. I spent four years down at Bellhaven kindergarten. That doesn't even make sense for an old, white biker guy, going down to an all-black school. I read to the kids, played with the kids, I colored with the kids. For four years, every Tuesday. That, again, was training to become a pastor in all ways. Going to jails, visiting patients. And you start putting all these pieces together and say, "What does that look like?" God was turning me into a pastor and I didn't even know it.

Rides to Work was the same way. I was still looking for things to do. A man from church called up and they needed somebody to drive people places. Well, I'd been driving some cars for a local Ford shop, so I could do that. I can go to the homeless shelters and pick up a couple people here and there. That'll keep me busy. I wasn't looking at that as ministry. I was thinking that would be a little extra money that would help around the house, because I wasn't making much money and was feeling down on myself. So I took that deal, a couple hours every day. And I started to see everything clearly in a vision from God. That this is more than driving. These people are homeless, these people are hurting, these people need help. So I looked at the lady who ran the desk, about a month in, and I said, "I want your job." And it's not because I wanted to be in charge. I didn't want the desk job; I'm not that great at it. But

I wanted her job because I see me being in the evangelism with the homeless, the poor, the sick, etc.

Several people called out that this was all leading up to me becoming a pastor. I didn't see it years ago. Then in 2013, something simple happened. I was caring for people and doing hospital and jail visits. I was thinking, "This is what pastors do. Why can't I marry people, too?" So I got my chaplain license and started learning how to marry people too. I've done twenty-one weddings—on-the-job training to become a pastor. So all these pieces were coming together. I was a care pastor for eight years. I didn't wake up one day and think, "I'm going to be a pastor." A friend said she saw that in me way back in the biker ministry era and that she's been dreaming of that for me.

Since I accepted the call, everyone I've spoken to has confirmed it.

Rudy Hears God's Call

Rudy heard God calling in his continued experiences in the coffee shop, and through that Rudy had to reach out to and help the next generation.

One thing that I realized is that, first of all, every business venture has a purpose. Sometimes the business venture is personal. And sometimes the business interest is collective. The coffee shop is collective. I realized at one point that when I really got to know these five twenty-two-year-olds, that I wanted to help young people realize their dream—as long as that dream not only helped them, but also helped someone else that they didn't know. And that's why the mission of this little for-profit coffee shop is to ultimately create employment opportunities in the coffee world. One is training others to be baristas. And the real, missional opportunity on this shop is our portable coffee shops. The goal is that we are going to get ultimately ten or fifteen of them on the streets in Houston, in parks, and we're going to launch a micro coffee business for young baristas in portable locations. So this primary location is a benefactor of the pop-ups all over the city. Imagine: A young barista could potentially make 150 to 200 bucks a day. That's good cash, no doubt about it. So they could end up with a real career, after it's all said and done.

Jordan Hears God's Call

Even as I was discerning where to commit to a body, I saw The Point's website. I felt a curiosity. I came and visited the church in April or May, and then in the summer I took a seminary class called A Missional Church. I saw what the church system was all about, and their missional DNA: what it means to be the church and how to love our community. It was exactly what I wanted to be a part of.

Jason Hears God's Call

Len was asked to participate in a roundtable about media in the church. Len mentioned the dream the two of us had been tossing around to an old professor of his, who responded by telling Len of a group who had been trying to get him to go to Texas to teach this same skill set—using media and art to create innovative worship design.

The group wanted to go digital and create media resources for the church at large. None of this looked the way Len and I had dreamed it would, but we could feel that God was whetting our appetite for something different. We both felt the call, and we were beginning to recognize how the call could come about.

The company wanted us to come lead them from print to digital. The CEO of this company flew to Ginghamsburg to attend worship. That weekend, there was a guest preacher. The sermon was about getting the lame man out of the house. He said, "You gotta have a pit crew," and spoke about the roles people needed to play in any God-given adventure. The roles were "investor," "innovator," "initiator," etc. There were Len and I, sitting there listening to this with our investor. At dinner after the sermon, the CEO looked at us and said, 'Could God be any clearer? I guess it looks like you guys are supposed to come to Texas.

A further confirmation of God's call was when Len and I were preparing to take on this new adventure. The very last design team we were a part of was a series the pastor had planned about getting out of the boat. "You can't rest on your past laurels. You can't stay in the boat," he said.

79

Tom and Sandy Hear God's Call

Tom and Sandy heard God's call to get out of their boat and go to China. They continued to hear God calling them across the water throughout their ministry work in China.

So at that point China's not in our minds at all. We're still working until 2004. We're just praying about what to do, and my nephew is going to China to teach English. My brother Paul says, "Hey, let's go together." So we said we would. That was an eye-opener. We went with his son, our nephew, to class. He's teaching English at a university, and we were on display because his students are learning English and they have to talk to us. That's their assignment. Some of them are Christians, so we got exposed to that.

While we were there we had the chance to hear some young people hearing the gospel for the first time and receiving Christ as savior in a completely different way than we were accustomed to in the US. Seeing the Holy Spirit work that way. When we got home from that trip, having been impacted by all of the events of that "vacation" we'd taken on a lark, we find out that my brother's oldest son and family are going to adopt a baby from China. So

*we're starting to see the Lord's big orange signs,
"China, China."*

Tom and Sandy describe their time in China ministering
to others.

---

*God spoke to us in steps, but you also have this
inner witness. Sometimes you don't get it, so
you think, "Wait, let's reevaluate this, think
about it, and pray about it some more." And
then sometimes that witness came after you
stepped through the door. We came home from
teaching or learning really tired. We went to
bed at eight o'clock unless a Chinese friend
called and said, "Can we talk? Can we go
to get tea?" And you knew right off that was
somebody's heart crying. And you said yes to
that. We said yes when we were dead tired, over
and over. But came back rejoicing for what the
Lord was doing. The guy who wanted me to do
the wedding, he's a friend. He's a pastor in the
house church, so he could've done that himself.
But this was a week before the wedding, so the
couple came to our apartment with him, and
we talked through it. We just learned to say yes
when things came to us like that.*

Chandi and Jamel Hear God's Call

Hearing God's call wasn't audible to Chandi and Jamel. Instead, they began to hear God through the relationships they were developing with others. Jamel never aspired to start his own clothing line, but because he was obedient to God in making himself a shirt, a movement started because others who were facing addictions and struggles wanted to wear a God Body shirt as well. As Chandi began to open up about her low self-esteem, other women encouraged her to share her story to inspire others. Hearing God's call happened to this couple as they said yes to the opportunities in front of them, with one step of obedience at a time.

Callie Hears God's Call

As I prayed and spoke with my spiritual director, I clearly sensed God telling me to step out of full-time paid work. That sounded crazy. I didn't know anyone who could work, who loved to work, who had job offers doing what they loved, and no kids or family needing high levels of care, but who didn't actually work. I wanted to dismiss the idea, but my spiritual director encouraged me to wrestle with why. The truth is, I was good at my job and placed a lot of my identity and worth in what I did and in doing it with excellence. If I didn't work, I had to face the question: Who is Callie apart from the job? And I had to do so in a new community meeting people for the first time. But the more I prayed about it, the more clearly I knew God was calling me out of the boat of familiarity and comfort and into the unknown of unstructured, unscheduled days, onto the waters of trust.

So I broached the subject with Roz, and my crazy, wonderful, courageous husband said I needed to do whatever it was God was calling me to do. I don't know if he felt guilty for making us move or like he owed it to me for supporting him in his new job venture, but he encouraged me to step out in faith and go for it.

Chapter Five Study Questions

1. When have you heard God's call inwardly? Outwardly? How have you discerned this call from God?
2. Have you heard a call that seemed to make no sense, though you knew it came from God?
3. In what ways does God give you your next steps or talk to you about your lifelong mission?

Chapter Six

Stepping onto the Water

Faith is taking the first step even when you don't see the whole staircase.

—MARTIN LUTHER KING JR.

"It's impossible," said pride.
"It's risky," said experience.
"It's pointless," said reason.
"Give it a try," whispered the heart.

—UNKNOWN

Then Peter got down out of the boat, walked on the water and came toward Jesus.

—MATTHEW 14:29B

Who knows? Maybe some part of Peter was hoping that Jesus would respond to his question by saying, "Nah,

Peter, sit back down in the boat and stay dry." Then Peter wouldn't be facing the prospect of doing something completely crazy, yet he could maintain the satisfaction that he was still "willing" to do whatever Jesus asked. Yet, there he was in the moment of truth. Would his faith be enough to get him out of the boat?

When we convert our words, thoughts, and faith into action, we are stepping out onto the water. We don't focus on the circumstances; we rise above the circumstances and focus our eyes on Jesus. When we think we can't do it, we're right: we can't—not on our own, at least. If we think we don't understand it, we're right: we don't—not on our own, at least. But Peter wasn't walking on water alone or in his own strength or understanding. Jesus was already out there. God doesn't call us on solo adventures or into areas we can wrap our minds around. He says, "Come *with me* into this mysterious work of the Kingdom that I have chosen for you." And when we face opposition, when we face trials and obstacles during our adventure, he's there.

Proper focus allows us to move in faith. Focus necessarily requires a blocking out of thoughts, concerns, or opinions that will get in the way of completing a task. As in the Martin Luther King Jr. quotation at the beginning of the chapter, walking in faith means focusing on that first step and not worrying about the invisible staircase ahead. Author Anne Lamott writes about her pastor's metaphor for acting in faith: she compares it to being on a dark stage and waiting for the next spotlight to appear, going to that spotlight, then waiting for the next one and the next one, never worrying about how the play is unfolding, whether the audience is enjoying it, or what exactly your role might be.[1]

Peter stepped out on the water, focused on Jesus. He couldn't worry about the purpose of his foray into water-walking, how impressed the guys back on the boat were going to be, whether he'd be able to walk on the water tomorrow, or if he would ever be able to draw large crowds by telling of this experience in the future. He heard Jesus' call, fixed his eyes on Jesus, and suppressed all other thoughts and feelings about what he was about to do.

While God is always at work behind the scenes, sometimes we must step out in faith before we see, in the real world, how God is supernaturally intervening. Perhaps nowhere in the Bible is this better illustrated than in Joshua 3, when the priests had to step into the River Jordan before the river stopped flowing so that the Israelites could cross on dry ground.

We live in a world where media and marketers send us many messages. It's estimated that Americans see thousands of messages each day. The goal is to appeal to us in some way in order to get our hard-earned money. Some of these messages are so strong, they compel us to act immediately. We can recite tens or hundreds of marketing slogans cued only by the company's name.

Gatorade, the thirst quencher, asks, "Is it in you?" When? Now!

Nike says, "Just Do It." When? Right now!

And Burger King: "Your way, right away."

The reason advertisements make their offers *now* is because *now* is their best chance to lasso potential customers.

What if I told you that there are times God uses the world's messages to reach Christians? In this case, taking action toward God's calling *now* really is important! While the reward for taking a risk is rarely immediate, if we don't begin to take the steps today we may never reap the rewards. So what are we waiting for? Are we simply allowing life to pass us by, or are we living our days with purpose?

In the movie *Dead Poets Society*, Robin Williams's character gives boarding school students a lesson in *carpe diem*. Williams plays an English teacher who takes his class into the hall near a trophy case. There he shows the students pictures of past heroes of the school. "All of these young men were as you are today," he tells them, "starting life with great promise. All of you will someday be as they are. They're all dead and so will you be. What do you think they would say to you? Get up close to the glass." As the class leans toward the glass, Williams, in a raspy voice, says, "*Carpe diem*. Seize the day, boys. Make your lives extraordinary."[2]

There are many times we put things off in life. I'll start that diet after the weekend. I'll exercise when it gets warmer outside. I'll get involved in service to God when the big opportunity comes. I'll read my Bible when I wake up early enough in the morning. Yet when the morning comes, we hit snooze. Or we pass by many small opportunities waiting for the big opportunity. We put things off all the time instead of seizing the day.

I remember having a long list of aspirations that I wanted to achieve before my daughter was born. I found myself working on projects around the house and goals in my personal life because I knew time was ticking and soon I would have one of the biggest responsibilities of my life. I tried to make the most out of each day. This taught me a valuable lesson. I shouldn't need a deadline to get things done or take a step of faith. There is no ideal time. I'm not guaranteed tomorrow. You aren't either.

Imagine if you lived every day with the goal of taking a step of faith. There's so much we can do for God's Kingdom today. This is exactly what one person did in the final minutes of his life in Luke 23:39–43:

One of the criminals who hung there hurled insults at [Jesus]: "Aren't you the Messiah? Save yourself and us!" But the other criminal rebuked him. "Don't you fear God," he said, "since you are under the same sentence? We are punished justly, for we are getting what our deeds deserve. But this man has done nothing wrong." Then he said, "Jesus, remember me when you come into your kingdom." Jesus

answered him, "Truly I tell you, today you will
be with me in paradise."

––––––––––––

The second of Jesus' last statements was one of assurance. "I assure you, today you will be with me in paradise." When the first criminal starts insulting Jesus, the second man rebukes him: "Don't you fear God even when you're dying?"

If you had one day left on earth, how would you spend it? If you've ever sat with someone who was leaving this life to go to the next, you know what a holy moment that can be. A few years ago, I made the trek to New York to spend a final day with my dad before he passed away from Alzheimer's. My dad looked at me and told me he loved me, and I got to pray with him. Neither of these things ever happened while we had lived together in our household. I'm glad we seized that opportunity.

Philippe Petit is a tightrope walker, and he is not afraid to take risks—that is, if you call walking across a wire stretched between the towers of New York's former World Trade Center taking a risk. In 1974, as thousands watched below, Philippe Petit made seven crossings of his cable stretched 1,350 feet above the traffic and concrete of Manhattan dancing, spinning, grinning, and even lying down in the middle.

Petit said, "I started putting a wire up in secret and performing without permission. Notre Dame, the Sydney Harbor Bridge, the World Trade Center. And I developed a certitude, a faith that convinced me that I would get safely to the other side. If not, I will never do that first step."

Tony Campolo, a sociology professor and preacher, describes a study of fifty people over the age of ninety-five who were asked what they would do differently if given the opportunity to live life over again. What do you think they said?

There were many answers, but three struck a chord with the majority of respondents: reflect more, risk more, and do more things that would live on after they were dead. These people didn't examine their lives regarding all the successes or failures *per se*, but rather by the risks not taken or what could have been.

What is the hardest part of activating adventure in our lives? It's usually taking the first step.

Recall the criminal who, in a moment while dying on the cross, asked Jesus, "Remember me." That criminal took a risk. In his final moments, he chose to put his faith in more than himself. He chose to put it in Jesus. It wasn't something he put off, but he did it right then and there. What if we lived every moment like it could be our last?

Tom Bulleit, a devout Catholic whose values and perseverance stem from his faith in God, grew up humbly as an orphan in Louisville, Kentucky. At the age of five, Tom was adopted into a loving family that believed in him and instilled in him a strong work ethic. His desire to make a difference in the world from a young age led him first to be a Marine Corpsman in Vietnam, then to earn law degrees from the University of Louisville and Georgetown University, and eventually to become a successful lawyer. Life was good, he was newly married, but he had a dream he could not shake. Tom traced his biological family roots to discover his ancestry, and the answer surprised him. Tom discovered that his great-great-grandfather, August Bulleit, was a bourbon distiller born in Louisiana, who had migrated to Louisville to make his small-batch bourbon back in the mid-1800s.

After further research, Tom began to consider resurrecting the bourbon brand. Many of his friends thought it was a silly dream. Tom's wife, Betsy, promised to help support him in his dream. In 1987, they began pitching proposals to prospective funders but discovered that bourbon was not a promising investment. Wine was the hot commodity in those years. After many attempts, Tom still hadn't gotten any investment on the hook. He and Betsy were discouraged, but they persevered. They decided to take the ultimate risk; they self-funded the entire project. While Tom was starting the business, he continued to practice law for another decade. Then, he gave up his lucrative career to invest time and money in bourbon.

One of his early lessons was that distilling bourbon is a slow process. Bourbon has to age for years before it can become consumable and competitive in the market. (Bulleit Bourbon ages in a barrel for a minimum of four years.) In those early days, the financial burden piled up, and at times, the stress of finances, a start-up business, and a new marriage were too much to bear. Still, Tom and Betsy didn't give up. Many of Tom's friends describe him as persistent. Betsy has a better word for it: maniacal.

Tom took the step of faith and never looked back for the boat. In 2005, Tom experienced a setback with colon cancer. It didn't stop him from going on the road in between treatments working to make Bulleit an international brand. Tom says, "I have been in a fox hole and on an oncology ward, and I have not found an atheist in either place."[3] Tom's faith and hard work ethic has brought him to where he is today.

Today, Bulleit Bourbon is celebrating its thirtieth year in business. The company grew in popularity to the point that Diago, the largest worldwide distributor of spirits, purchased it. Tom remains the face and global brand ambassador of Bulleit Bourbon.

Bulleit Bourbon just completed its new distillery in Shelbyville, Kentucky, outside of Tom's hometown. The price tag for the project was $115 million. Thirty employees oversee the bourbon-making process with a starting capacity of 1.8 million proof gallons annually.[4] Bulleit even made it on the big screen with mentions in motion pictures and TV shows such as *The Expendables*, HBO's *Deadwood*, and Netflix's *House of Cards*.

Today, Tom is approaching eighty with no signs of slowing down. He still travels the world sharing the message of Bulleit Bourbon. When asked about his retirement strategy, Tom replies, "Death." Tom is building something that will outlast him and that he will eventually leave to his kids and grandkids.

We each have only one life, and the only person who will ever live it is you. Life isn't about playing it safe; it's about going on a God-adventure that involves ups and downs. The only way that adventure can start is by taking the first initial step.

Angie Steps onto the Water

At that point when I woke up, it was a call to prophetic ministry. I had no idea what that meant, so I spent the rest of the day researching. What is prophetic ministry? How do you do it? So I started trying to understand the call. What would I be doing? What would it look like? I was processing. What do female prophets do? Are there female prophets? Am I just supposed to be like a male prophet? I finished my undergrad work in three years, and then came to Dayton to attend United.

Tim Steps onto the Water

If Tim is honest, he's a little terrified at the prospect of going back to school to become a pastor. But he knows God has called him and equipped him in his experiences over the past twenty years and that he will help Tim translate that into the necessary academic work in the years to come.

I know what I'm here to do, but you never know what you're going to go through. You didn't know whether the water was going to be rough or smooth. It was very scary to step out and write this first document, the call document. That was a big step.

Going up in front of people, having been out of school for thirty-five years. Even then, I went to tech school. I didn't write papers. I don't have a college education. It's very scary still right now.

Rudy Steps onto the Water

Perhaps more than most, Rudy was raised to step out of the boat.

One thing is for sure, my daddy raised me with a mantra. He always told me, "Nothing beats failing like trying." I have really never been risk-averse. I've always believed that you have to step out of the boat in order to walk on the water. It's always a walk on the water. I don't care what the venture is. Whether it's starting a church, opening a coffee shop, going back to school, or launching a business, all of them are walks on the water.

So I borrowed about $150,000 and started making the renovations, buying the equipment. About $200,000 to $240,000 later, we now have a shop. And that's not including the land and building.

The mission is to create employment opportunities and training opportunities for younger adults, in many cases who might be in transition. Some of these folks, if they weren't working with me, they would be homeless. But because they're working with me, they have income, they have opportunity, they have a future.

―――――

Jordan Steps onto the Water

―――――

When I saw the job description, I could see potential, but in the moment I had to call my dad and say, "Dad, can I do this?" Someone to back me up and believe in me in ways I couldn't see. To say, "Yes, you got this." God *was going to equip me, but I needed the affirmation. That came in through mentorship relationships, too.*

———

Jason Steps onto the Water

———

Len was a Texas native, so leaving Ohio meant homecoming. For me, it was another story. In addition to leaving friends and family, my wife, Michele, and I were engaged at the time and had our wedding planned in Ohio! Wanting to give the church ample time to put a transition plan in place, I gave eight months' notice.

There were plenty of moments during these eight months that I thought twice about stepping out on the water. I loved the work I was doing at Ginghamsburg. I was earning a good income at a church that was flourishing. I would be leaving all this to go to a company that knew it was dying.

Nonetheless, we stayed focused on what we felt called to do, left Ginghamsburg, headed to Texas, and began our work there.

———

Tom and Sandy Step onto the Water

When our nephew's adoption took place, we went with them for a second trip. It was a completely different experience but just as impactful. We started talking to the organization that our nephew was part of. At that point, I [Tom] was almost sixty-five. I said, "Hey, what can we do? Do you have any openings for people like us?" And the man said, "Well, as a matter of fact, we have a summer teaching program." We signed up for that in 2005. China won't allow you to be a full-time teacher over sixty-five, so we signed up for summer teaching, six weeks, in China. That was our first baptism by fire.

Having been there doing the summer teaching, a job opportunity came up, and we applied and were interviewed, and went through a multitude of papers—a psych evaluation and personality tests—and we were on track for taking that job. We had Skype interviews and phone interviews. And at the very end of that, they offered us the position. One question that hadn't been answered to our satisfaction was how much money we were going to need to raise. And they came back with an amount, and we looked at each other and thanked them *for their time, and we were absolutely, hopelessly disappointed. We had to have $3,000 a month. Now we're retired. I was retired at the time and Sandy was considering retiring. And we thought we'd been through this whole process for nothing. Set our hearts up for this, told our families the potential and prayed about it for nothing because there's absolutely no way. We thought there must be another ministry, another door would open somewhere else. We went to bed heartbroken.*

The miracle was the next morning. We both got up and said, "We're going." Just like that. And we didn't know where the money was coming from or anything, but we both had the inner witness that God was saying, "Just do it." So that was the breakthrough.

We stepped onto that water. We had some expectations as employees and volunteers. We had our own heart-leading from the Lord. But we really had to humbly accept the leadership that was in place there. And we waited patiently to abide by their rules, and I feel like that was part of standing on the water, just waiting. As we were seen as faithful and obedient to the leadership and the authority over us, doors opened for ministries I can't explain in just a few minutes' time.

We were making new friends at a Chinese church. Everything's in Chinese, so we don't understand what's happening. We had people come around us who were translators and so they translated everything for our benefit. We get to be really good friends, and we go to their Bible studies and small group. That was awesome. Tom performed a wedding. The couple came from unbelieving families, but they were both followers of Christ, so they wanted a Christian witness, not just the standard Chinese wedding celebration. We did English Corner, where we came and did an English lesson for young people who had been tasked by their church to reach their colleagues and their classmates. We were just the foreigners who would get people to come in, but then they did ministry. If you say you're going to do an English Corner, Chinese people just show up. You get a dozen people just by word of mouth. So we had two English Corners going on while we're working at this guesthouse and going to Chinese church.

Most of the Americans there are going to the Beijing International Church. It's a big church, a thousand people every morning. It's very much like church here. You go to a big church here, it's virtually the same. So we prayed about that, and God said, "No, you're here to be with Chinese people. Don't spend all your time with Americans." And in every case, those doors opened allowing us to step into people's lives. Stepping onto the water was not as hard as stepping into people's lives. But that's where discipleship happened, that's where salvation came to souls, that's where the work of the Lord really blossomed. It was awesome.

Chandi and Jamel Step onto the Water

Chandi and Jamel's first step of obedience as a married couple was to begin sharing their experiences with others. The first opportunity to do so came through a series of Facebook Live posts dealing with various common issues that couples often face. As they began to share, they were surprised by the popularity they gained and how much interaction they received from friends and complete strangers. One day while Chandi and Jamel were online, someone suggested they should have their own talk show. They responded, "Why not?" At first, they thought it was a little silly, but as they thought about it further, they saw the need others had to hear their story. They began a monthly talk show at The Point called *Grown Conversations*. Next, they began to share their testimony at a number of churches. Although it was scary to air their dirty laundry in public, they saw others getting real with themselves and their significant others and realized what God had been calling them to.

Callie Steps onto the Water

I had the hard conversation with my boss to let him know I wouldn't be working for NCF Kentucky from Dayton, Ohio. I helped the staff transition, packed up our house, and said my goodbyes to everything that was familiar. I was nervous, but I had this confidence knowing it was God calling me onto the water. So on June 1, 2014, I entered this new season.

It's never too late to seize the day and take that step. How will you seize the day? Ways to do so, both small and large, are all around us. For example:

- Expressing appreciation to those around you.
- Hugging, calling, or texting your children or parents.
- Taking the first step to take better care of your physical body.
- Speaking words of empowerment and encouragement to someone who needs to hear them.
- Starting a new habit or service to God.

- Starting a business.
- Finishing a degree you started but left behind.

Today is the day.

Chapter Six Study Questions

1. What can we do to focus on God to the exclusion of our own worries, fears, and desires to control the circumstances?
2. Describe a time you have stepped out on the water. What enabled you to do so? What was the result?
3. What could obstruct you in answering God's call?

Chapter Seven

Sinking and Rescued!

Being content to walk with God brings peace in the midst of uncertainty. It brings wisdom in the unknown. It brings contentment in any situation and grace in every circumstance. It brings mercy and forgiveness in sin and blessed assurance in condemnation. It brings freedom from captivity. Walking with God brings light and air into the pit, as God reaches down to rescue us when we fall.

—TERESA SCHULTZ

But when he saw the wind, he was afraid and, beginning to sink, cried out, "Lord, save me!" Immediately Jesus reached out his hand and caught him. "You of little faith," he said, "why did you doubt?"

—MATTHEW 14:30–31

Peter's doing it! He's walking on the water. Then, with a fresh gale of wind or a cold burst of waves, he shifts his focus and gets that sinking feeling many of us are familiar with: "I'm in over my head! I don't belong here! This isn't working!" The doubts and discouragement creep in. It's easy to forget that it was never *us* doing the amazing thing on our own to start with. Instead, we question how we're going to continue doing the amazing thing "alone." And we begin to sink.

When we take our focus off of Jesus, even for a split second, we start to feel alone. We see the waves around us, and we focus so much on sinking—on failing—that it becomes a self-fulfilling prophecy. We start to question and doubt. Why did we ever try to step out of the boat in the first place?

So where did Peter go wrong? Peter *doubted*. The word for "doubt" in Greek, *distaz*, doesn't necessarily mean unbelief but can be better translated as trying to go in two different directions.[1] Acting in faith requires a singular focus. Doubt divides our focus and causes us to fall. Peter's body was on the water so long as his focus was Jesus. It was a miracle! But, for a split second at first, Peter's mind refocused on the water, the waves, the wind, and probably (by contrast) the memory of the boat and its relative comforts. His focus couldn't be in both places at once; it was split, and he was led in different directions.

I remember sitting in a McDonald's about eighteen years ago, eating a Big Mac and fries and listening to a recruiter tell me how I would travel the world and gain valuable life experience in the Marines. He was right, but what he didn't tell me was how terrible boot camp was going to be for twelve and a half weeks at Parris Island, South Carolina.

When you step out and take a risk, you might find yourself signed up for something you didn't bargain for. If you knew the entire plan ahead of time, there is a chance you wouldn't pursue it in the first place. I have experienced this many times in my life. I knew that my parents wouldn't be able to afford to send me to college. I began to look at the military reserves as an option to earn money through the GI Bill while gaining valuable experience most eighteen-year-olds wouldn't get. Money for college wasn't the sole motivator; I also wanted a challenge to do something I had never thought I could do.

When you're in USMC boot camp, the last thing you want to do as a recruit is to stick out like a sore thumb. Unfortunately, I had no hope of blending in as the shortest recruit of sixty-three guys. For the first few weeks, my four drill instructors made it their job to make my life miserable through a little game they played. Any time the other sixty-two guys messed up, I was the one who took the punishment, and, as a result, was pushed to my physical limits. For example, if someone didn't make their bed or was the last to get out of bed, the drill instructors would yell my name and tell me to get down on the ground and start doing pushups. Luckily, my experience wasn't like that the entire time, but I did think, "This is not what I signed up for!"

My world was disrupted and I felt displaced in an unfamiliar place with people I didn't know. Things worked out, but it was much harder than I anticipated; and, at the time, I wanted to be somewhere else.

When I stepped out of the boat of my hometown and joined the Marine Corps, I didn't necessarily view it as a calling. However, I discovered something while I was there. I needed God more than ever in those times of loneliness. As I shared with some of the fellow recruits about my faith in Christ, something happened that I wasn't expecting: others started to come to me for prayer requests, I became the lay leader of my platoon, and my drill instructors would ask me to pray before everybody went to bed. I discovered my "toughness," but, more importantly, my call into vocational ministry by providing spiritual care and counsel for others. Boot camp and my military experience has become some of the best preaching material. My experience in the Marines challenged my mental toughness but also strengthened my faith in how God can use me in the most difficult circumstances. I got that sinking feeling many times but always found God's arm reaching out to me when I looked to him.

Whenever we take a step of faith, there will be doubts. However, we have the choice to focus on the doubt or focus on the faith. When we feed doubt and long for the safety of the boats we once knew, we give in to defeat. Doubt can come from a thousand places. We may hear the voices of family members, teachers in grade school, or old acquaintances: "You'll never amount to anything." "You're not smart enough." "You will never change." Doubt can also come from the people who don't understand an act of faith. "Why would you do something so foolish?" "You'll never pull that off." "Better to just keep on doing what you're doing." "You have it so good as it is."

It's hard to know exactly what triggered Peter's doubt, but I know what goes through my mind when I walk in faith. I fight my own demons of self-doubt and fear of failure. Meanwhile, some of us hear voices from a hurtful past or voices of negativity from others around you.

On the other hand, some people self-sabotage because of the fear of *success*—because the pressure of God's unknown is more frightening to them than the misery they are accustomed to. The minute they start taking positive steps in their lives, they get scared that they might succeed at something. They believe they don't deserve the success, that they won't know how to handle it, or that they'll screw it up.

Yet another possibility is that we become complacent, lazy, and arrogant, thinking we've done it all ourselves and forgetting that we need to focus on Jesus at all. Perhaps what first distracted Peter was not fear at all, but simply the desire to look around at his surroundings and see what "he" had done instead of continuing to focus on the one who had called him.

Doubt calls us back to the boats we left behind to follow Jesus. In the Old Testament, the children of Israel experienced this doubt when God delivered them from their Egyptian captors. God delivered them from lives of slavery, but they longed to go back to Egypt where their lives were predicable rather than continue wandering in the desert, dependent on God for their next steps. In Egypt, though life was cruel, they knew what to expect each day. When we take the step of faith, we have to make a conscious decision not to look back. Our focus can't be in two places.

A partner to doubt is worry. Worry is one of the worst enemies anybody can have, especially church planters. One survey regarding worry indicated that 40 percent of things most people worry about never happen, 30 percent of what we worry about has already happened and therefore is too late to change, and more than 20 percent of what we worry about are problems that are beyond our control. In the end, this leaves less than 10 percent of what we worry about to situations that we can influence. There are things within our control, but obviously, many more circumstances are outside our control, including those in our past.

When we do begin to sink—as we all will from time to time—Jesus is there to rescue us just as he was there to rescue Peter. This is the great thing about acting in faith. When we are focusing on our faith and the next step God has placed before us, we will feel most intimately connected to God and most alive. But even when we fall, we still get to experience God's saving grace and be reassured of his love for us. Jesus didn't let Peter flounder and slosh around in the water until he could barely take it before he reached out and rescued him. Immediately, when Peter called out, Jesus reached out his hand and rescued Peter. We can expect no less.

Acknowledge the disappointment. As you take risks, you will inevitably have disappointments. If we never talk about it with friends, in accountability circles, or with spouses, we hold onto it instead of getting rid of it. But there is something that happens when we are real before others and God. Confession is therapeutic. The truth will set you free—even when it's painful!

Let it kick your butt—but only for a moment. Sometimes it's OK to put your head under the covers or bury it in the sand—for a moment. But while this is normal, it shouldn't be something we consistently do. It's good to remind ourselves of the promise that "weeping may stay for the night but rejoicing comes in the morning" (Psalm 30:5b).

It's not the end of the world. This too shall pass. We always have the promise of a new day with new opportunities before us. Loss and disappointment are very much real emotions, but they can't be an excuse for not taking the next opportunity or God-adventure right in front of us. Every season in life comes with twists and turns, but disappointment is not a perpetual season we have to find ourselves in.

Tomorrow is a new day. Life goes on, and the pain doesn't last even though the scars do. They are reminders of lessons we can learn and carry with us for the rest of our lives to help others for God's glory.

Zapp put Dayton on the map in the late 1970s and early '80s and has since traveled the world. Zapp was a cutting-edge funk group that used their famous talk box and sound alongside Prince and Cameo. Zapp's fame quickly spread with multiple gold albums and a number-one hit on the R&B charts with their single "Dance Floor." The group had ups and downs, reinvented themselves, and contributed to Dr. Dre and Tupac's famous single "California Love." All seemed right in Zapp's world as they released a greatest hits album that went platinum.

But tragedy struck on April 25, 1999, and Zapp would never be the same. Band member Roger Troutman had established a solo career and was managed by his brother Larry. Tensions had mounted over money, the family business, and Roger's success as a solo artist. Larry shot his brother with four bullets and then turned the gun on himself. The family was left in tragedy. But that didn't stop them.[2]

Most people would have packed up everything because of the tragedy, but not Zapp member Terry Troutman. I have had the pleasure of knowing Terry because he and his family are members of my church. Terry's faith grew in the midst of the tragedy, and he decided to take a step out of the boat once again by getting the band back together and bringing in new faces with the same funk sound that put them on the map. Today, Zapp performs over one hundred shows a year. I had the opportunity to join them for one of their shows, and it was quite the experience, almost like I had been to a worship celebration: over and over again they gave glory to God. It doesn't erase the pain and tragedy they went through, but they didn't give up on what God has put them on the earth to do.[3]

Many times, when disaster strikes, the first thing that happens to us is that we become paralyzed with fear, and the temptation to continue forward with our call and our God-given journey can quickly go by the wayside. I have learned from Terry what true perseverance in faith means. Taking that first step of faith doesn't mean we won't get knocked down or start to sink, but if we don't give up, God is always there to reach out his hand and rescue us.

It is inevitable that we will face failure from time to time when we follow Jesus. Yet these moments can bring us nearer to God, reminding us who he is and reinforcing our faith. Moreover, God calls us to his work in part because he knows we will need to rely on him thoroughly for our strength and ability.

Angie Sinks and Is Rescued

Very frequently I doubted. I was older than most of the students in school. I felt that I was too old, I was female, I am black. I had an identity crisis. But my call was always affirmed, even though I constantly questioned it.

Tim Sinks and Is Rescued

I knew what my gifts were. But I guess my biggest doubts were about being responsible for all these lives, all these jobs, all this transportation, all the paperwork. I can get by, but I didn't have very much self-esteem about being the director of a whole nonprofit. That's not really my gig. Helping people's my gig. So I was pretty scared about that part of it. But to do the job God gave me, I knew I'd have to learn and be able to do this other part of it, too.

Rudy Sinks and Is Rescued

Every now and then, you'll look away from Jesus, and you'll start to sink. And that sinking feeling is just a result of disconnecting from the one who gave you enough courage to take the step in the first place.

Every six to eight months over the last four years, I had an "oh, shoot" moment. "Oh, shoot, what have I done? You mean I'm gonna have to spend some more money? Oh, shoot, you mean this is gonna have to go even deeper than just a little coffee concept that I

114

was thinking earlier?" The answer across the board was yes. Every coffee shop owner that I know told me to not do it. Every restaurant/ food and beverage person I know told me it was hard and a nightmare. But the funny thing is, when I asked all of them would they do it again, they all told me yes. So I knew there was enough in it for them to want to do it again but not necessarily enough to convince a pastor they liked to take a risk. Even now, when people ask me, "Would you do it again?" I'm telling them, "Yeah, I would. Matter of fact, I think I'm going to do it again in Indianapolis. Then I'll come to Dayton and show you how to do it!"

Jordan Sinks and Is Rescued

Being able to lead a team of adults was one of my biggest fears. I was twenty-four at the time. "What is a millennial going to teach?" I made that excuse.

Another of my biggest fears was what the relationship would look like across ethnicities, across socioeconomic status. I had to come into a completely different neighborhood and learn.

I had to humble myself. I had to get out of my pride and my fear. I got more emotionally and spiritually healthy, dealing with my own wounds and fears. I needed healing to trust the voices that believe in me and trust in my leadership. I did personal counseling, cognitive behavioral therapy to deal with anxiety, talk it out with people I needed to talk it out with.

I reached some honesty with myself and God. As I was making space for God, he was able to come in and speak to who I really am.

Jason Sinks and Is Rescued

When Len and I arrived in Texas, things weren't exactly as we'd expected. Two weeks in, we found out that this other guy had been promised that he was going to be in charge. We had specifically been told we were going to be in charge. We had left a place of cutting-edge thinking to a place that was very institutional. Had we given up our best opportunities by leaving Ohio? At Ginghamsburg, we had already been reaching churches through conferences. Now we were going to have to start at square one to begin establishing relationships, reaching out to potential clients, all while making sure we could somehow get paid to do so.

Nonetheless, God reassured us this was where we were supposed to be. Eventually, Len and I realized that we could move faster together on our own and began our own company in Texas called Lumicon.

Tom and Sandy Sink and Are Rescued

We'd been asking for God's leading and call for years and assumed it was going to be to a Muslim community somewhere. That dream was over, we thought, and here we were going to be working with Asians. That kept coming up as, "Well, God, why did we pray for this for all these years and it didn't come through?" But whatever, we're going to go to China.

As we're starting through this process, my dad has a massive heart attack. We're thinking, "OK, God, are you saying to put an end to this whole interview process?" But that wasn't his plan. I thought maybe my family needed me, but God said he would take care of that as well. And my dad's still going. He's healthier now at eighty-five than he was at seventy-four!

Then, just as we're leaving, Tom is diagnosed with prostate cancer and needs surgery. This was 2006. We had already taken this job in Beijing. We accepted a call to go for three years. I [Tom] had an appointment to go for surgery. The surgery we were scheduled for, the doctor said, "You really don't want this." So they changed the type of surgery. It went well, and we were back in China in two or three weeks to start our job.

We did have times of sinking once we were there too. Doubts. Those were times of illness. If you're sick there, you don't go to the doctor's office; you go straight to the hospital. You would keep your garage cleaner than some of these places. We went to Thailand three times with the organization for a conference. The water was always bad. We had bacterial infections every time. Hundreds of people gathered, including the speakers, were getting sick. We'd get back to Beijing and go to the hospital. They gave us an antibiotic and it went away.

There were lots of health challenges. And yet, even one health challenge, Tom's cancer, gave us the chance to connect to doctors at a nearby cancer hospital where he could be a witness. They were just delighted to have me [Tom] as a patient. I'd go over there for a blood test, a routine test, and the doctor would take me to the place where you pay and get checked in. He said, "Don't worry about that, just come with me." He'd take me up to some floor where he knew the nurses, and they took the blood, gave me the results, and I didn't pay a penny. And even when I did pay, it was ten dollars instead of the hundred dollars it should have been. We went to the hospital a number of times. We actually still have an account at Beijing United. We get a discount.

We also terribly failed with communication at times. We still have trouble with our Chinese. But we also had some successes. So there was sinking and floating back to the top. We had been to church on Easter Sunday. That's the day people get baptized in droves. The next morning I was listening to a Chinese woman tell her story to one of my coworkers who understands Chinese very well. And she's counting off on her fingers how many people. I assumed she was talking about how many people in her family had been baptized. That was my assumption. But really she was listing how many people in her family had had to go to the hospital with food poisoning. So I'm listening, smiling, and nodding, thinking, "This is wonderful!" But no, this was people going to the hospital.

We met people on the bus, the subway. They want to talk in English. It is so easy to witness. They want to know what's with Americans. What do you believe? Why are you here? The doors just open; you don't have to pry them open.

Don't look down, just keep looking up.

———————

Chandi and Jamel Sink and Are Rescued

The steps of obedience for Chandi and Jamel haven't been easy. They have been tempted to give up at times. Each time they share, they face the temptation to give into the fear of others' judgment. Their own insecurities about how their message would be received have almost stopped them from sharing it. Originally, Chandi thought she would simply share their story through writing; she didn't know God was calling them to public speaking.

Recently, Chandi wrote a song that her daughter has recorded. The song lyrics speak about living through the pain, pushing through in faith, and writing your own story.

Callie Sinks and Is Rescued

I loved having this time to move and get settled in Dayton and meet new people, but then what? I would start wrestling with my purpose and identity. I kept checking with God to see if now was the time to start working again. I was getting involved at church, volunteering in the community, and meeting all sorts of new friends, but didn't God need me working somewhere? I kept trying to remind God that statistically the longer a person is without work, the harder it is to get a job. But God kept telling me to wait and keep trusting him. Each time I looked down at how silly what I was doing seemed in the world's eyes, God reminded me that his ways and plans are better than anything I can imagine or dream up. He also kept telling me to enjoy this season because I'd miss it when it was gone.

Chapter Seven Study Questions

1. Can you remember a time when doubt interfered with something God had called you to? Where was your focus initially, and how did it get split?

2. What can you do to maintain continual focus on God's call on your day, your year, or your life?

3. Do you rely on daily practices to keep your mind from doubt and worry? If so, what are they?

4. What is more likely to shift your focus away from Jesus' call: actual fear of failing or just desire to return to the comfort of your boat?

5. Have you experienced God's rescue when your doubt was causing you to sink? Describe this experience.

Chapter Eight

Living a Walking-on-the-Water Life

If three steps are taken without any other motive than the desire to obey God, those three steps are miraculous; they are equally so whether they take place on dry land or on water.

—SIMONE WEIL

And when they climbed into the boat, the wind died down. Then those who were in the boat worshiped him, saying, "Truly you are the Son of God."

—MATTHEW 14:32

As far as we know, Peter never walked on water again in his life, either during his time with Jesus or afterward. It also wasn't the only time he lost focus and began to sink spiritually. Peter had many other walking-on-water moments in his discipleship and ministry, ultimately becoming enormously influential in the early Christian church.

A life of walking on the water with Jesus can take many forms. Every day, we can find something God asks us to do. The call can come from the Holy Spirit working through Scripture, a member of the clergy or our Christian brothers and sisters, nature, books and art, or from a voice we actually hear. Whether the call feels mundane (like extra caring for your family when it's needed), or awe-inspiring (like starting a new ministry with a large outreach base), the goal is to present ourselves each day for God's call, expecting to hear from him, freeing ourselves from the need to understand the big picture of God's call, and preparing ourselves to convert our belief into active faith.

Peter may have taken the first steps on the water, but the impact on those still on the boat can't be overlooked. The other disciples make a confession at this point that Jesus is the Son of God. Peter's faith helped shape that moment for them. When we decide to live a walking-on-water life, the sheer act of stepping out of the boat, even aside from whatever the concrete results are, impacts not only us but those who are still in the boat. Our faith can become contagious.

In John 10:10, Jesus describes the abundant life, the life we were intended to live. This life is not reserved for only a few of us, but is meant for each of us who desires to follow

Jesus onto the water. Every day of this abundant life presents new challenges, opportunities, and risks. God is a God of newness. God's mercies are new every morning, though his promises remain the same. God wants us to grow in our risk, hard work, faith, and the miraculous presence of the Holy Spirit.

Living a walking-on-water life means not becoming fixated on past success and risk-taking faith, but instead remembering God's faithfulness to call us out on the water again and again. Celebration is merited and worthy of our time. But when we fixate on a successful moment, we can get stuck in a celebration dance like a football player after scoring a touchdown. We forget that the game isn't over, regardless of our most recent success. We must use God's past faithfulness to repeat the cycle, pushing off from shore, facing our fears, and stepping out of the boat, no matter what lies ahead.

Many leaders and organizations get stuck in trying to relive their glory days, even when they have long since passed, and they consequently grow complacent. They remember the way things were instead of looking at the opportunities and risks in front of them. I experienced this very thing as a young church planter. I was presented with the opportunity for our church to go multisite through an urban restart. The church was Epworth United Methodist Church, which has sent out over a hundred people into full-time vocational ministry. They were the flagship church in their day, and everyone wanted to attend there. But when we merged with them in 2011, the church had less than sixty in attendance, those who attended were seventy years old on average, and the building was in disrepair.

Epworth was stuck celebrating their former victories. The parishioners retold stories of the glory days when their three-hundred-seat sanctuary was filled—balconies included—and Sunday school classes were the attraction of the day. As Epworth's neighborhood transitioned, the church divorced and isolated itself from the community. Attendees commuted to the church because they no longer wanted to live in the surrounding neighborhood. Twenty years earlier, several in leadership wanted to relocate the church to the suburbs, but the vote never passed because of the abiding affection for the church building that many of them had funded to build.

Meanwhile, when our Embrace Church leadership team considered the merger, a few of our folks advised against it out of fear. They were comfortable worshipping as a new church in a movie theater and didn't think it was possible to be one church in two locations, especially with one location in a sketchy neighborhood. Massive problems stood in front of us. I began to challenge them to focus on the faith instead of the fear. We got on board for the merger.

If planning a parachute drop was challenging, doing the restart of a dying church nearly killed me. We faced the challenges of two urban churches: funding ministry on the margins of the city, a building that needed repairs, and a community that needed to regain hope of what God could do in a declining area. After a few years, Epworth became a community center as we reached out to the neighborhood, built a positive culture among the seasoned saints, and did out-of-the-box ministry. Embrace and Epworth both began walking on water.

There are times in life when it becomes easy to give up and throw in the towel. If you ever played a sport or an instrument when you were a kid, what you probably heard often times ringing in your ears is that practice makes perfect. How often are we perfect at something? We may be good—but perfect? It seems like no matter how hard we try at things, we can't ever be quite perfect because, despite being able to control ourselves, we can't control the outside variables or the outcome. What happens when you try something over and over again and feel like a failure? Think of a marriage that is in constant turmoil, a never-ending search for Mr. or Mrs. Right, business startups that never take off, repeatedly getting passed over for a promotion at work, the up-and-down struggle to get out of debt, or the continual battle to maintain a healthy lifestyle.

When we experience continual failures in any area of our lives, the temptation to give up grows stronger. No matter how hard we work or try, the results never seem to come quickly enough for us. Even when we work a plan or strategy, prepare harder than anybody else, the results can still disappoint us. So what's the answer?

The answer is the gift of stubbornness. When I was discouraged early on in my ministry, a pastor friend of mine told me—only half in jest—that stubbornness is actually a spiritual gift I should pray for. When we have done all we could have done, the greatest gift we can give ourselves and others is to not give up.

Tennis star Andre Agassi once said, "Success and failure are so often the result of outside factors, things beyond our control, so you need to keep your mind on the few things you can control. Learn to love the process, the work, and disconnect your ego from the results. The earlier you learn this, the more peaceful you'll be, and peace, not success, is the goal."[1]

The truth is, I know many people who have given up right before they experienced a breakthrough. Sometimes, the question we have to ask ourselves is how we define success or failure. Failure doesn't have to define our lives; it's a moment and doesn't have to be a state of being. Ninety percent of the battle we fight is simply getting out of bed, giving our best efforts to what God has called us to do, and leaving the results to God.

John Wesley, who founded Methodism in the seventeenth century, learned this lesson of always taking the next step, not getting hung up on past failures, and letting God make sense of the steps. As one of the most influential Christian leaders in the history of the church, Wesley's genius was building smaller groups. Though not the most powerful preacher compared to his contemporary, the great evangelist George Whitefield, Wesley knew how to organize and empower the laity of his day. At the time of his death, Wesley had "294 preachers, 71,668 British members, 19 missionaries (5 in mission stations), and 43,265 American members with 198 preachers."—and today, there are about 30 million Methodists worldwide.[2] How about that for a résumé?

But what's just as interesting as that litany of successes is that one of Wesley's biggest regrets turned out to be one of his greatest legacies, despite the fact that he wasn't able to see it in his lifetime. In his life, before his actual conversion experience in 1738, Wesley described a mission trip to Savannah, Georgia, as a complete and utter failure.

The year was 1735 when he set sail for Savannah to minister to the Native Americans. While on the ship, they were facing dangerous storms and Wesley feared for his life but took notice of his shipmates, the German Moravians, who were singing and praising God. Wesley realized something was missing from his spiritual walk. While in Savannah for three years, he fell in love with Sophia Hopkey but chose not to continue the relationship because of interference with his ministry. Hopkey married another man. Then Wesley, due to emotional turmoil, denied Hopkey communion in worship, and Hopkey's husband took him to court and filed a complaint, which eventually culminated with Wesley heading back to England.

Wesley says, "I went to America, to convert the Indians; but oh! who shall convert me? Who, what is He that will deliver me from this evil heart of mischief? I have a fair summer religion."[3] Wesley, feeling like a failure, could have given up. Here he was, leaving and feeling like he didn't accomplish anything. However, God used that encounter with the Moravians to do something in Wesley's heart. He kept in touch with some of those Moravians on the ship, and they invited him to a worship gathering on Aldersgate Street in London on May 24, 1738, where Martin Luther's Commentary on the Book of Romans was read. After Wesley heard that commentary, he explained in his journal, "I felt my heart strangely warmed. I felt I did trust in Christ, Christ alone, for salvation; and an assurance was given me that He had taken away my sins, even mine, and saved me from the law of sin and death."[4] Wesley found the healing and wholeness he needed by accepting the invitation of these friends who witnessed him what genuine faith looked like in the midst of a storm.

John Wesley's greatest failure ended up propelling him into God's most exceptional work for his life. What may look like a failure and a mess on the surface can be an ingredient for a miracle when we are humble enough to cry out to God. Sure, Peter took the step out of the boat like Wesley, but like Wesley, he found himself quickly drowning when he took his eyes off Jesus and looked down. Too many times we focus on our problems, naysayers, and what's around us instead of looking to Jesus. Wesley rebounded by going to that worship gathering. Wesley could have easily given up, but if he had, he would have missed out on the breakthrough of a lifetime. Almost 250 years later, a statue of John Wesley was erected in Savannah,

Georgia's Reynolds Square close to the parish house where Wesley once resided.[5]

One of the greatest revivals in history took place out of the movement Wesley started, but he also inspired other aspiring entrepreneurs such as Arthur Guinness. Guinness lived during a difficult time in eighteenth-century Ireland, with widespread disease caused by pollution, leaving the drinking water untouchable and resulting in many deaths. The alternative drinking option to water was alcoholic beverages. Alcoholism began to run rampant and led Ireland down the devastating period called The Gin Craze. Ireland became so plagued with drunkenness that Parliament banned the importation of liquor in 1689. Much like the response to the Prohibition in America, bootlegging became popular and there were "gin houses" where people made gin in their bathtubs. It only added to the problem. Many wanted to create a safer alternative to gin, so some turned to brewing beer. The beer was lower in alcohol content, killed germs, and provided nutrients. The early pioneers in brewing were, ironically, monks, Christians, and aspiring entrepreneurs such as Guinness.[6]

When Guinness went to church one Sunday morning at St. Patrick's Cathedral in Dublin, he heard a preacher who had started a great revival in England. That man was none other than John Wesley. While there is no record of what Wesley preached that day, it had a profound effect on Guinness. Based on Guinness's actions, one can only guess it was Wesley's message of generosity, helping those on the margins of society, and spreading scriptural holiness across Ireland. Guinness founded the first Sunday School in Ireland, gave to those in poverty, and challenged those in the wealthy class to do the same. Guinness began more than just his now famous brewery; he began a legacy that his children carried on, which bettered the lives of their employees and which they believed would make for a better Ireland.

All of this because one man dared to dream. The beer and wealth were only a tool God used by helping those in Ireland. Guinness made the decision to be different than his peers and took the first step of faith that left a legacy.

Angie Lives a Walk-on-the-Water Life

For me, the interesting thing about faith is that each experience builds on the next. You can look back and say, "I was a cocaine addict, and I never thought I'd begin to get healthy and take care of my family." But I did, and Jesus built on that and was always building on the next step. I just remind myself none of it means anything apart from God.

Today, Angie is a talented teacher and preacher. She began a Celebrate Recovery worship and recovery community at the Fort McKinley campus of Ginghamsburg Church. Angie's passion is for others to experience the freedom she has had for the past twenty-seven years. By continuously taking the next step out on the water, Angie has become a valuable resource to the community, especially in the Dayton area, which is one of the US cities hardest hit by the heroin epidemic.

God has truly raised Angie up for such a time as this. In addition to Angie's recovery passion, she has started her own nonprofit called Nurturing Dreams and Visions Inc., a home for troubled boys. The vision is "to inspire young men to live life without 'limits.'"[7] Angie plans to open a home for young girls in the future as well. The independent living facility offers life skills in cleanliness and home care, dining and table etiquette, grocery shopping, cooking and meal prep, laundry, STD prevention and sexual education, job readiness, GED prep and counseling, budget and money management, and college or trade prep.[8] Angie never would have guessed that by answering God's first call to recovery, she would be taking the first step on the path to beginning ministries and nonprofits. God has taken the mess of her life and turned it into a miraculous message. Angie continues to take steps of faith on the water as God uses her testimony in Dayton and across the state of Ohio.

Tim Lives a Walk-on-the-Water Life

Everything I've done at that church, from walking in there sixteen years ago to the initial shaking hands and greeting people, is about walking on the water. When I started with the biker ministry, I was always a follower and God made me a leader. People would be riding their motorcycles and say, "Hey, let's go get something to eat." And I'd be like, "Hey, let's go help somebody." I kept saying that, and everyone kept saying, "Well, why don't you do something about it?" God started making me a leader. And then I helped teach kids' choir, then kindergarten, then security. I've done everything under the sun in that church, except clean toilets. God was doing on-the-job training for me being a pastor, even though it started sixteen years ago. I claim all of it because it all intertwines.

Rudy Lives a Walk-on-the-Water life

My wife, Juanita, joined forces with me on day one. She stepped out of the boat too. She was self-employed when she was twenty-one. She didn't have any risk-aversion tendencies either! She said, "Okay, let's go get it." From there, we began to really work on taking step after step. Over the years, we decided that our investment model would be real estate. And then we ended up pastoring a church in the downtown area that did what? Invested in real estate! So we realized along the way that you have to do what you're gifted to do and allow those gifts to be used for the Kingdom. And it works out. It's not always comfortable. But it works out.

―――――

Jordan Lives a Walk-on-the-Water Life

―――――

The OpenTable ministry was my launching pad into this community. One of the ways was asking God, "What are you already doing here?" and being open to God showing me people in this community where God is already at work.

A couple years ago, I would never have imagined where I am today. These pastors in my life were able to fight for my call. I see this in you, when I didn't see it myself. Now I'm in a place of confidence in who I am, hearing God's voice and discerning where he's leading me.

―――――

Jason Lives a Walk-on-the-Water Life

Years later, Len and I began a second company called Midnight Oil, and eventually I took over sole ownership. Although there have been periods of slower growth, in total, this company grew quickly.

Jason has seen God's call fulfilled again and again. He estimates that he has spoken to about 15,000 church leaders in the past 20 years. He has "secret worshipped" in approximately one hundred churches, providing the churches with feedback after. He has coached around one hundred pastors. These small- to medium-sized churches have been able to make significant changes to their worship design at a fraction of the cost of hiring a full-time worship or media design staff member.

Tom and Sandy's Walk-on-the-Water Life

Tom and Sandy don't believe in retirement. When Tom turned seventy-five, they moved back to the States and resumed their mission work in their hometown of Trotwood, Ohio. Here they build relationships with neighbors, tutor the refugee and immigrant populations, and serve as care pastor and prayer warriors at The Point. The call of Jesus to step out onto the water is not reserved for young people or people in the prime of their careers. The call is for people of all ages. In fact, retirement means more time for what God is calling a person to do. All of the significant figures in Christian history, including many biblical characters, did some of their greatest work after what we consider "retirement age."

Callie Lives a Walk-on-the-Water Life

I kept lifting my eyes off the waves and refocusing my view on Jesus because as long as I was focused on him, I could enjoy the season I was in. I basically did everything I would have done in retirement but with the energy of a thirty-year-old. I built amazing friendships and got to grow through serving in ways at church and in the community that I never would have had time to if I were working full-time. And a year to the day later, on June 1, 2015, I began working at United Theological Seminary as Senior Director of Development. The timing couldn't have been more right as I entered that new role. My first year working at United was incredibly challenging, but I was ready to walk with God on the water through that next season after seeing him prove again and again his faithfulness in the last season.

Helping Others out of the Boat

If you have ever decided to step out of the boat, you also have an obligation to spur others to step out who still find themselves sitting comfortably in the boat. If I were in the boat with the rest of the disciples, of course, I would have been shocked to see Jesus walking on water—but then to see Peter doing the same thing? I hope I would have said to myself, "Why not me?"

Living a walk-on-the-water life isn't just about getting up after sinking, having the commitment and courage to get out of the boat the next time, or walking in a private communion with Jesus. Living a walk-on-the-water life is also about encouraging others to do the same. Peter served as a disciple-maker for the other disciples the night he decided to get out of the boat. Peter spent the rest of his ministry after Jesus' resurrection encouraging others in their faith.

A modern-day example of living a walk-on-the-water life can be found in one of my close friends and mentors, Pastor Mike Slaughter. After becoming a successful youth pastor in Cincinnati, growing his youth group to about two hundred people, his district superintendent called him and told him to pack his bags because a church was opening up for him. As Mike and his wife, Caroline, were making the drive from the growing city of Cincinnati to the rural farmland town of Ginghamsburg, Ohio, with a population just shy of 5,600 residents, they were a bit frightened. The introduction meeting didn't go well; the church was traditional, and Mike was a hippie in those days, having been saved in the Jesus Movement. Mike's long shaggy hair and beard were a turnoff to the people of Ginghamsburg.

After the introduction meeting, Mike's district superintendent apologized and said Mike and Caroline didn't have to come to Ginghamsburg Church; however, he went on to say that if they decided stay, he believed a great miracle was in store for them and the church. After taking some time to pray, both Mike and Caroline accepted the position.

The budget in 1979 was $27,000, and the attendance was ninety. Mike jokes that he grew the attendance to fifty-eight after just a few months. One morning in prayer, Mike decided to take a stroll directly behind the church building where there was a field. As he prayed, Mike received a vision and saw 3,000 people in worship. Mike believed that he had heard from the Lord. The next step was action. Mike and Caroline formed a small discipleship group in their home, and the church took off from there.

Many are now familiar with Mike's story. The church did grow to beyond 3,000 in attendance, has committed itself to being the hands and feet of Jesus in other parts of the world and at home, and has done vital, life-transforming ministry for 38 years. Whenever Mike feels God speak to him, he doesn't waste any time but jumps out of the boat.

Mike has made it a key point in years of preaching and ministry to encourage others to do the same. He has often said, "Walking in faith is ready, fire, aim—not ready, aim, fire. You activate your faith by stepping out, and God will direct your path." Having stepped out of his "boat" at Ginghamsburg after thirty-eight years by "retiring" and moving on to other areas of ministry, many have recently had the opportunity to reflect on Mike's impact in their lives.

———

Because of Mike's commitment to the Sudan, I signed up for a mission trip to distribute mosquito nets over there. The passion for service I felt stayed with me back in Dayton, and I'm now in my fifth year of helping to run a tutoring program for African refugees in the Dayton area and organizing a winter clothes drive and community-building events for the refugees. Seeing Mike's faith walk called me out of the boat—it was foundationally important in me discovering and investing in my mission work! —Benjamin Holmes

———

I remember a sermon long ago when Mike told us that Peter wasn't a failure when he sank while trying to walk to Jesus on the water. At least he had tried. The other disciples just sat in the boat and watched. I decided that day to get out of the boat, and I'd deal with the consequences as they came. This mind-set has led me to run for public office, start a business, and take many other risks that I've felt God is calling me to. Everything isn't always sunshine and roses, but at least I'm not just sitting in the boat watching other people reach for their dreams. —Kate Kyle Johnsen

---

One particular quote that has been mentioned multiple times and has changed my view of Christmas and missions is Mike's famous line, "Christmas is not your birthday." This shifts our thinking from receiving to giving to more than just our families, and about how we can be more like Jesus and give to those in need locally and globally. —Ryan Manger

---

Pastor Mike has encouraged me to step out on the water several times over the years, but the one that is foremost in my mind happened during the "Dare to Dream" series. His sermons clarified and expanded my thinking and made me consider writing a life mission statement. I discovered that my life mission statement is rather simple: "to inspire." This has enriched and helped focus my ministry of teaching art—my life's passion and gift. I was forever changed by

*that, and it has helped me to grow closer to God
and expand my ministry. I am so very grateful
for Mike's teaching in my life. —Trish McKinney*

These reflections demonstrate the profound impact stepping out of the boat and living a walk-on-the-water life can have on other disciples of Christ.

Entrepreneurs and risk-takers can be motivators and empower the next generation of leaders. Bishop Milton Wright founded what today is United Theological Seminary in Dayton, Ohio. It was Bishop Wright who encouraged his sons to take flight, but while they were in high school, they started their entrepreneurial attitude in a bicycle shop and printing business. It was in high school where they spurred on the work of a classmate, a sixteen-year-old boy by the name of Paul Laurence Dunbar. They not only encouraged him in his poetry, but they printed his work to get it out to the general public. Despite dying at the young age of thirty-three due to tuberculosis, Dunbar is known today as one of the greatest African American poets.[9]

In this case, you could say that it took a few dreamers to take a chance on another dreamer. Some dreams would have never seen the light of day were it not for the prodding and pushing of others who encouraged someone to step out of their own boat. Proverbs 27:17 tells us, "As iron sharpens iron, so one person sharpens another." Risk-taking faith doesn't happen in isolation; it occurs in the context of friendship and community. As we grow in our faith, we sharpen another person's faith, and it takes place in reciprocal relationships. There are countless times I have mentored young pastors and church planters where I have learned just as much from them as they have from me. There is always that early pioneer who is willing to get out of the boat first. Everybody else may think about it, but only a select few will follow and do the same. There are times we need to extend our faith to others and believe in them when they don't believe in themselves and make way for them to step out.

As for me, when I planted my first church in Lexington, Kentucky, I was right on the heels of a divorce. My spouse had committed adultery and left me devastated. I felt like retreating back to my hometown and admitting defeat. How could I answer the call to go into vocational ministry as a church planter and stay in the same city where it all happened? I stepped out of the boat but quickly looked down and wanted to climb back in. It was a mentor at the time, Aaron Mansfield, who was a pastor of a local church where I did my seminary internship, who believed in me when I didn't believe in myself, when others doubted me. Aaron gave me the opportunity and encouragement to preach monthly at his church. If it weren't for him, I wouldn't have planted my first church or gone on to do anything else in ministry. Aaron provided me with the example of extending faith to others.

Many times, our biggest naysayers and doubts are within. If we've made mistakes, fallen short, and missed the mark, we think somehow that these things disqualify us from doing something in this life. Not only is that contrary to the Scriptures; it's also contrary to how God has used women and men throughout the history of time.

Don't let the mistakes of the past dictate the step of faith you need to take today! There are too many people who feel like failures, and because of that insecurity, they never attempt to do anything greater than themselves.

God's call is not often the safe and easy route, but once you live into it, you can't stop halfway. The living-on-water life is not a comparison to someone else's call or journey. God has designed you uniquely and the only one who can live out that calling is you. Don't covet another person's calling, gifts, talents, and abilities. The life God wants you to live is specifically designed for you.

Peter got the hint and followed Jesus. The apostle Peter didn't stop taking risks after he preached his first sermon, but remained obedient even to death. His walk-on-the-water life shows us how we can develop a strong faith and allow God to accomplish his will through us, one step at a time.

Chapter Eight Study Questions

1. What phase in this cycle do you see yourself in now? Pushing away from shore, spooked, stuck in a boat, asking for God's call, hearing God's call, stepping out of the boat, or sinking?

2. Name at least one area—recently or in the near future—where you feel God might be calling you to step out of the boat.

3. In what ways can you continue to live a walk-on-the-water life each new day or new season?

4. Who in your life lives a walk-on-the-water life and can be there to encourage you to do the same? Who can you encourage to get out of their boat?

NOTES

Chapter One

1. Craig L. Blomberg, *Matthew*, vol. 22 of *The New American Commentary*, ed. David S. Dockery (Nashville: Broadman Press, 1992), 233.
2. Ibid., 233.
3. *Groundhog Day*, directed by Harold Ramis (Culver City, CA: Columbia Pictures, 1993).
4. This recently hit home for me when a mentor pointed me to a book by Jeff Manion and his sermon on the same topic. Jeff Manion, "The Land Between," YouTube video, 40:42, from a sermon posted by NewHopeOahu, February 25, 2013, www.youtube.com/watch?v=nn5cvHhXdvk.

Chapter Two

1. Craig L. Blomberg, "The Development of Jesus's Ministry," *Matthew*, vol. 22 of The New American Commentary, ed. David S. Dockery (Nashville: Broadman Press, 1991), 234.
2. Urban Meyer and Wayne R. Coffey, *Above the Line: Lessons in Leadership and Life from a Championship Season* (New York: Penguin Press, 2015), 41.

Chapter Three

1. Sheryl Lynn, "Francis Chan Goes into Detail With Facebook Employees on Why He Left His Megachurch,"

The Christian Post, June 29, 2017, www.christianpost
.com/news/francis-chan-goes-into-detail-with-facebook
-employees-on-why-he-left-his-megachurch-190136/#
.WVjDD_a7wNQ.facebook.

2. Ibid.
3. Francis Chan, "Structure," We Are Church, accessed July
   4, 2017, www.wearechurch.com/structure-1.
4. For more on Tim's work, see Nancy Bowman, "Miami
   Agencies Combine Efforts for Rides, Jobs," *Dayton Daily
   News*, February 15, 2017.

Chapter Five

1. 1 Kings 19.
2. Dennis M. Campbell, "Chapter 3," in *The Yoke of
   Obedience: The Meaning of Ordination in Methodism*
   (Nashville: Abingdon Press, 1993), 53–54.
3. Fran Walsh, "Professional Comic Turned Preacher: Rev.
   Jerry Herships," United Methodist Communications,
   February 28, 2013, http://www.umc.org/news-and-media
   /professional-comic-turned-preacher.

Chapter Six

1. Anne Lamott, *Traveling Mercies: Some Thoughts on Faith*
   (New York: Anchor Books, 1999), 84.
2. *Dead Poets Society*, directed by Peter Weir (Burbank, CA:
   Touchstone Pictures, 1989).
3. Rosario Picardo, and Tom Bulleit (Bulleit Bourbon), in
   discussion with the author, July 18, 2017.
4. "Bulleit Distilling Co. Cuts Ribbon on New $115 Million
   Distillery," Distillery Trail, March 14, 2017, www.distillery
   trail.com/blog/bulleit-distilling-co-cuts-ribbon-new
   -115-million-distillery/.

Notes

Chapter Seven

1. Craig L. Blomberg, *Matthew*, vol. 22 of *The New American Commentary*, ed. David S. Dockery (Nashville: Broadman Press, 1992), 253.
2. David Burke, "Zapp Band Continues on Funk Trail," *Quad-City Times*, April 23, 2015, www.qctimes.com /entertainment/zapp-band-continues-on-funk-trail /article_7922b186-901a-5b16-a554-a453104dca06.html.
3. Terry Troutman (Zapp Band), in discussion with the author, April 13, 2017.

Chapter Eight

1. Rana Florida, "Your Start-Up Life With Andre Agassi: Playing Big," HuffPost, September 10, 2012, www .huffingtonpost.com/rana-florida/your-startup-life-with -an_b_1866970.html.
2. Leslie K. Tarr, "John Wesley," *Christianity Today*, accessed June 28, 2017, http://www.christianitytoday.com/history /people/denominationalfounders/john-wesley.html.
3. John Wesley, "Journal of John Wesley," Christian Classics Ethereal Library, accessed June 28, 2017, http://www.ccel .org/ccel/wesley/journal.vi.ii.vii.html.
4. John Wesley, *Journal of John Wesley*, vol. 1 (Charleston, SC: Self-published via CreateSpace, 2013), Kindle edition.
5. "John Wesley Monument," Visit Historic Savannah, accessed June 28, 2017, http://www.visit-historic-savannah .com/john-wesley-monument.html.
6. Stephen Mansfield, *The Search for God and Guinness: A Biography of the Beer That Changed the World* (Nashville: Thomas Nelson, 2014), 52.
7. Angela Edwards, "Who We Are," Nurturing Dreams and Visions Inc., www.nurturingdreamsandvisions.com /about, accessed July 20, 2017.

Notes

8. Angela Edwards, "Brochure," Nurturing Dreams and Visions Inc., www.nurturingdreamsandvisions.com/our-brochure, accessed July 20, 2017.
9. Richard Stimson, "Paul Laurence Dunbar: The Wright Brothers Friend," The Wright Stories, accessed July 20, 2017, www.wrightstories.com/paul-laurence-dunbar-the-wright-brothers-friend/.

CPSIA information can be obtained
at www.ICGtesting.com
Printed in the USA
FFHW012027190319
51155432-56614FF